Art Museums

Gerhard Mack

Art Museums
Into the
21st Century

**With a Contribution
by Harald Szeemann**

Birkhäuser – Publishers for Architecture
Basel · Berlin · Boston

This book is also available
in a German language edition
(ISBN 3–7643–5962–5)

Translation from German: Michael Robinson

A CIP catalogue record for this book is available from the Library of Congress, Washington D.C. USA

Deutsche Bibliothek Cataloging-in-Publication Data

Mack, Gerhard:
Art Museums: into the 21st century/Gerhard Mack.
With a contribution by Harald Szeemann. (Transl. from German: Michael Robinson).
- Basel; Berlin; Boston;
Birkhäuser, 1999
Dt. Ausg. u.d.T.: Mack, Gerhard: Kunstmuseen
 ISBN 3-7643-5963-3 (Basel…)
 ISBN 0-8176-5963-3 (Boston)

Design: Karin Weisener, Birkhäuser Publishers
Production: Atelier Fischer, Berlin
Cover Design: Atelier Fischer, Berlin
and Karin Weisener, Birkhäuser Publishers
Reproduction: Bildpunkt GmbH, Berlin
Printing: MEDIALIS Offsetdruck, Berlin
Binding: Ghaddar & Schulz, Berlin

© 1999 Birkhäuser – Publishers for Architecture,
P. O.Box 133, CH-4010 Basel, Switzerland
Printed on acid-free paper produced
from chlorine-free pulp. TCF ∞
Printed in Germany

ISBN 3-7643-5963-3
ISBN 0-8176-5963-3

9 8 7 6 5 4 3 2 1

Ecce Museum: Much Chaff, Little Grain

by Harald Szeemann

A prophecy by Nostradamus (1503–1566) that has so far attracted little attention, and a rather more precise one by the Lower Bavarian shepherd and millstone-grinder Mathias Lang, known as Mühlhiasl (he prognosticated from 1780 to his death in 1825), not only foretold that it "would no longer be possible to tell man and woman apart", but that before the Third World War "many buildings like palaces will be built – and then there will be stinging-nettles growing out of their windows". In other words before the apocalypse predicted by Nostradamus for autumn 1999. Mühlhiasl does add the further detail that the palaces will be built for "soldiers", but as military budgets are being cancelled and cut everywhere, and armies abolished, he must mean museums when he says palaces. And this is due to happen between the Second World War and the Third, which is still ahead of us, in other words between "Hister" (= Hitler) and another catastrophe merchant.

Of course there had been earlier museums that were open to the public, in London (1753), in Kassel (1779), in Paris, as a consequence of the Revolution, but the real flood of museums for modern art did not begin to surge over the Western world and Asia until the period of economic recovery in the fifties. Education, culture, art, architecture – right-wingers, left-wingers, even the Greens can find a common cause. Plots were made available in unlikely places, credit was set up, and we had yet another museum building, outwardly an envelope announcing the architect's articles of faith, and more or less suitable to house the works. Very often the building was so expensive that there was very little funding left for later activities. This was the simplest way of ending the argument that exercised people greatly in the sixties: about the ambiguity of the museum that on the one hand isolates creativity from life, and on the other hand offers protection and scope to the fragility of artistic creation. Yes, even artists' protests about unduly ingenious architecture have quietened a little, although Baselitz's manifesto in particular still has some validity today. He demanded pure walls that nails can be hammered into, with good toplighting and neutral floors, a notion that was of course sparked off by the shoe-box museum and the art gallery type that emerged during and after the First World War – in parallel with concert-halls, whose acoustics are still praised. Indeed, it can be argued that the best exponents of modern museum architecture may often take very complex detours, but still come back to this principle, starting with the work of art, designing a space on a human scale, creating frontality, and paying increasing attention to light. But the examples in which unity is produced by reflecting on the parameters derived from art are few and far between. The dominant feature is still the architect expressing himself fully, becoming a sculptor, seeing the building as a piece of self-realization, in other words relating so-called "artistic freedom" to himself in the first place. Purists and placers of emphasis, bores

and meddlers, are creating work alongside and against each other, as long decreed by the acceptance of stylistic simultaneity, something that has been lived out for us in art since the twenties, in the dialectic of the conflict between two unequal brothers, like Constructivism and free formal invention. What Kandinsky identified as an ethic of artistic impetus and called "inner necessity" is now personally claimed by every architect who builds a museum, often with disastrous consequences – galleries in the Louvre style that make it impossible to encounter any of the images as they always require the viewer to turn through 90 degrees (Hamburger Bahnhof in Berlin), silly floor structures that can't support a barrel vault, and lamps fitted at such a dizzy height that changing a bulb becomes a high-wire act (Deichtorhallen conversion in Hamburg). Or squares are multiplied *ad infinitum*, so that the windows providing side-light become the actual exhibits (Kunsthalle in Hamburg), Doric temple porticoes and grass-green top-lighting grids (Staatsgalerie in Stuttgart), rooms so high that even very solid dividing walls are reduced to looking like cardboard (Kunstmuseum in Wolfsburg), doors that are too low, lifts that are too small, table structures under the skylight that cut into any upright format – compensated for by curved, photogenic marble forms in the entrance (museum in Santiago de Compostela), light-chimneys as aids in small spaces and as a sculptural burden for the ceiling in large ones (Thyssen Collection in Madrid, with pink walls to boot, and in the new Moderna Museet in Stockholm), and however beautiful the ramp may be, the spaces are equally unusable (Museum of Contemporary Art in Barcelona). The list could go on for ever. But let us not forget that even Frank Lloyd Wright's Guggenheim spiral in New York is actually a corridor running around an empty space intended for a mobile – and as soon as a large picture by Rothko is hung on one of the wall modules the work starts to suffer, and the slanting floor is less than ideal for primeval housing like the igloo.

Whether negatively in terms of application or assessment (from the point of view of art) or – and here it comes – positively, it is certain that building a museum today means just as much for an architect as building a cathedral used to. Some are also fortunate enough to be able to build both, and then in each case the top-light may come from a diagonally-cut cylinder.

There is one architect who underwent an initiation by building museums, on his own behalf and for us. Renzo Piano (b. 1937) is one of the few who, how else can I put it, has never stopped learning since the Centre Georges Pompidou in Paris was built (1971–1977), that spectacular cultural machine in the former Les Halles quarter. It turned what used to be Paris's stomach into its head. The Centre, with its technical innards turned outwards, is certainly a magnificent structure, but it is not particularly suitable for works of art. Gae Aulenti did redesign the interior of the collection area in the eighties, and Renzo Piano worked over the spatial problem for the *galeries contemporaines*, but exhibitions, permanent and temporary, always have something unsatisfactory about them here. The presence of air-conditioning units and fire alarms above the works is tiresome, and the artificial light and trade-fair felt are less than uplifting. But they have never stopped people from coming to the building in hordes. However: this high-tech establishment is in need of a total overhaul after only 20 years. Piano then built two buildings for the De Menil Foundation in Texas: the main building (1982–86) to house the large Modern collection and works from cultures outside Europe, and then a jewel in the form of a pavilion for the work of Cy Twombly (1992–1995). Here, as in the museum opened last year for the Beyeler Collection in Riehen, Piano has listened to the works for which the spaces were intended. The floors are neutral, the skylight is fitted to the roof in a most ingenious manner; in Houston it consists of four layers of differing degrees of transparency, a white metal grid, electronically controlled solar deflectors, a skylight and finally a white sail. In the Twombly pavilion a tripod module to determine the volume of the rooms in the square structure was enough, but in the Riehen museum the rooms, which are constructed specifically for the works – particularly clearly in the case of Monet's water-lily triptych – and the casually parallel quality of the four load-bearing walls encourage visitors to explore and experience; this is a walk through a collection of personally chosen and exquisite works that are woven into the light. Not that the architect can be said to have effaced himself. The north-south direction, the eastward opening, the choice of materials and the handling of light mean that visitors are not forced round a course, but that they constantly find themselves within an entity suggesting a profound understanding of the existing reality and proclaiming a fertile co-operation between the client/collector and the visitors.

A complete contrast with this generous and introverted architecture, which places itself in the tradition of geometrical notions of space dating from Mies van der Rohe, is Frank O. Gehry's fluently sculptural architecture for the Guggenheim Museum in Bilbao, a building full of surprises in the alternation of undulating centrally-planned buildings and floral-style toplights, mixing fish-shaped, swinging, extended galleries and classical, box-shaped galleries, ramps and walkways, with an abundance of straights and curves, of indentations and bulges, of things visible and invisible, of surroundings included and excluded: the bridge, the harbour area and the river. The atrium is like a monumental version of Kurt Schwitters's Merzbau, made possible only by today's technology. Schwitters – like Gehry – conquered his three-dimensional universe in an unorthodox fashion, with bridges and oscillations. In his day, his ideas could develop into bold structures only by using roofing-slats, chicken-wire and plaster, but now, thanks to Gehry, a cathedral of erotic misery becomes a shining, dithyrambic triumph. And from the outside the titanium-clad plasticity of the building is like a great burst of sound, and Gehry's actual gift to the Basque country, which has now proved its cultural autonomy above all over Madrid and Barcelona with this brilliant achievement, despite a wretched economic situation and 25 per cent unemployment.

But however great Gehry's achievement may be, the collection, bought from a very few sources, and consisting of a few Spanish and European, but large numbers of American works, is poor, with a few exceptions. There are three hideous women's bodies by Dine, bad Warhols, an unsatisfactory LeWitt wall, the usual Kiefers, Schnabels, Basqiats and Burens, and a meagre Beuys collection. Only Richard Serra's steel sculpture "Snake", winding its way over more than 30 m, can hold its own against the extremely long gallery in the shape of a fish without tail and fins, but without any direct frontality. Lawrence Weiner's inscription REDUCE, over four metres high, is brilliant and subversive as a message, but it is from the Panza Collection. Thanks to Gehry, Janus-faced neo-colonialism has realized the boldest sculptural architecture of our century in Bilbao, but it has also shamelessly betrayed any auratic quality. One can only hope that once the initial curiosity is satisfied the stream of visitors will not dry up but will find increasingly exciting material in the constellation of galleries.

After these extreme positions, I should like to mention just two less spectacular examples.

The new Kunstmuseum in Lucerne tends to the traditional, with six rows of four spaces that are the same size and three larger ones, with toplighting in a combination of artificial light and daylight, which can be controlled individually. The computer simulation shows high, light rooms, white boxes, although the openings connecting them are on the small side. Walking through the building site gave an impression of a neutral sequence of spaces that could be used in a large number of ways.

The building for Ingvild Goetz, realized by Jacques Herzog and Pierre de Meuron in Munich in 1991/92, is definitely a private museum, a subtly conceived structure only 24 by 8 m in area, with an entrance through the office and archive and two exhibition floors with three and two galleries. Light is managed by lateral glazed bands, which make it impossible to look out because of the way they are doubled up. Human scale, isolation, the cancellation of time make the building perhaps the most consistent, intensive, calm place for confrontation with art, particularly of the most recent period.

It is not that I prefer the one type or the other, the quiet approach or the lively, sculptural one. The diversity is a sign of flexibility and wishful thinking. Mühlhiasl is right: before the Third World War, when the world was being catalogued and globally networked, an enormous number of palaces were built, some reticent, like discreet country houses in the 18th century, and some symbolic, like Bomarzo. The great difference between these and earlier palaces is that no one lives in them. They have opening times, they are available to the public, and they are housings or showcases for works of art with an aura that now have a patina, or have even been recreated by iconoclasm. This is my body, this is my blood, this is my museum, whether it is privately or publicly financed, whether it is successful or not, whether it is necessary or not. There is nothing to stop museums from multiplying. Obviously I hope that some are afflicted with the "stinging-nettles", and that others aren't. Obviously I have long since replaced the church with the museum. But what will the museum be replaced by some time? There is one museum per 9,000 inhabitants in Switzerland. Just think about it...

Time Rediscovered

by Gerhard Mack

A metal girl gets out of a car, makes a gorilla take a diamond out of her mouth and uses it to blow up a museum. That's how the Icelandic singer Björk chose to let off steam in the video clip for her CD "Army of Me". This funny story is in fact addressing a serious matter. There have long been complaints that museums keep art safe, but rob it of its life. They started as soon as the first public institutions appeared. In 1796, in his "Lettres", the critic Quatremère de Quincy described the museum as "a wax wilderness, like a temple and a salon; a cemetery and a school". He went on to say that art could live only as part of public life. He took Italy as an example. This was just three years after the Louvre was successfully opened to the public. And it didn't sound very different even a good century later. Filippo Marinetti called libraries and museums "cemeteries" that should be destroyed in his first Futurist manifesto in 1909. In 1923 the Russian Constructivist El Lissitzky declared: "We are no longer prepared to tolerate the exhibition gallery as a painted coffin for our living bodies." And Paul Valéry, writing two years later in his essay "The problem of the museum" summed it up like this: "Painting and sculpture (...) are orphans. Their mother is dead, their mother, architecture. For as long as it was alive, it gave them their place, their purpose and their limits."

Björk puts a new accent on these doubts. Her clip is set in some museum of contemporary art. Its galleries contain pictures by the iconoclastic Modernists of our century, whose *raison d'être* was always to smash tradition: the picture, the object, the perspective of the space and with them, the totality of memory, the present and dreams. It is possible to take the video gag seriously and see it as a symptom: by destroying the museum and its bright, white galleries, the young woman with metal teeth is putting an end to the Bauhaus style's long-lasting will to be recognized; she makes this built expression of Modernism into a historical memory. The museum rejoins time, and life begins with the passage of time. A young man was lying in state in the bombed museum like Shakespeare's Juliet in the family vault. The explosive charge detonated right next to his head and woke him from his sleep. A pious hope: the time of the princes is past, and today women rescue their lovers from their long, long sleep.

The museum boom, which has kept many cities in Europe and the USA busy building new museums since the seventies, is reaching another climax today: important museums by high-calibre architects opened in Bregenz, Basel, Bilbao, Los Angeles and Stockholm within a year. The concert hall was completed as the first phase of Jean Nouvel's Culture Centre in Lucerne, revealing the exterior shape of the art gallery. The New York Museum of Modern Art held a competition for a large-scale extension (fund-raising campaign for 400 million US dollars), and most of the leading younger and middle-aged architects were invited to enter. Japanese architect Yoshio Taniguchi's suggestion is to be built. But the

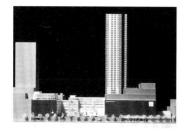

The winning design for an extension to the Museum of Modern Art in New York by Yoshio Taniguchi, Japan: photograph of the model with view from 54th Street, including the sculpture garden.

Taniguchi's model: view of the sculpture garden and museum tower.

Structures obstruct space: early wood sculpture by Sol LeWitt.

design with the most far-reaching implications, because it was most consistently oriented towards the future, was provided by the Basel architects Herzog & de Meuron. It is therefore presented in detail, together with the new Tate Gallery in the former Bankside power station in London, which has reached a crucial building phase and will be available for the curators to start their work from May 1999.

The eight projects are all different in volume and function. The Kunsthaus in Bregenz has no collection, and is intended above all for touring exhibitions. The Fondation Beyeler's private collectors' museum with its 2,700 m² is the size of a single exhibition floor in the classical museum area of the new Tate Gallery. The museum is not the first priority in the Lucerne Culture and Congress Centre, whereas in Bilbao it gives the whole town a new centre. The Getty Center with its five institutions towers over the city and bay of Los Angeles like a castle, but the Moderna Museet crouches almost ashamed between the barracks that still exist from a former military island in the middle of the city. Despite this variety, the various projects seem to stake out a terrain that reveals the possibilities of modern museum building. In the best case, even the choice of site identifies a tendency. Björk's video clip suggests a starting-point: the return of life, of time and transience is linked with a farewell to the spatial concept of the "white cube", which has excluded time as biomorphic factor.

If you read Donald Judd's early art criticism or texts by Dan Graham, then it is clear that the "white box" developed directly from later Minimalist artists' confrontation with the exhibition space. The question of what this space is and how art relates to it was finally answered by abolishing it as an exhibition space and redefining it as an artistic space. Art interventions now implemented the spatial claim that Abstract Expressionist artists had made with their gigantic canvases in three dimensions. The device used here was the infrastructure of the exhibition rooms, which has been paid scarcely any attention before. Dan Flavin mounted fluorescent tubes that he bought from the DIY centre in galleries, using them to replace the existing lighting. Sol LeWitt built timber structures that blocked up the space and were intended to be recycled as firewood afterwards. Art was ephemeral from the outset here, completely limited to the present and the exhibition. No one wanted it to last any longer, as an object to be bought, for example. The absolute present was reminiscent of the self-referential circular movement with which Abstract Expressionist artists tried to escape the linearity of Modernism and our arbitrary end in death. Pollock's line-spaces are the clearest example of this dance around the canvas, circling aimlessly, a meditative self-immersion in the language rhythms of Jack Kerouac's Beat ballad "On the Road" and Allen Ginsberg's poetry.

It is a commonplace that art, especially in enthusiastically materialistic America, has a transcendental dimension that is equivalent to religion. In the "white box" museum concept this enhanced present is centred on perception. The Judaeo-Christian religious sphere has conceded world-making status to seeing, from Genesis to the perception of Christ in mysticism, though not necessarily in a material sense. It is much more a question of being kept comfortably and safely together in a pure present with a partner, thrusting forward into a space and time of which scientific and technological measurement are unaware. The celebration of perception in the concepts of Minimal Art and the "white cube" gives an echo of this absolute. Transcendence shifts from the object to the process. To use a word in Friedrich Schlegel's sense, it becomes "transcendental".

It is no coincidence that museum buildings working within this context chose to address light, with its double set of metaphors based on religion and enlightenment. Take Peter Märkli's "La Congiunta" museum for sculptor Hans Josephson in Giornico on the St. Gotthard railway line as an example: the light pouring in from on high, the darkness below, the basilica-like nave and the niches fitted in like side altars all evoke religious moods. However, the bronze sculptures draw these towards a theme that defines Josephson's work as a sculptor: the archaic element in the history of man, his ecstasy and suffering, his chtonic existence, his orgies of destruction and his moments of peace. These are fragments of a salvation-history whose saviour is no longer recognizable. This object remains visible, and binds perception. Seeing does not circle around itself. To a certain extent it is a pre-modern form of the sacred, though of course it is aware of the alienations of Modernism. Peter Märkli's concrete envelope challenges this object and places it on-stage.

Peter Märkli's museum for the sculptor Hans Josephson "La Congiunta" in Giornico in Switzerland flourishes on material and light.

Peter Zumthor is different. His Kunsthaus in Bregenz takes light as its subject from the very first associations onwards. The hazy light over Lake Constance and the Alps flows around the glass cube on the lakeside like an early mist around a Japanese lamp in the branches of a tree. This theme is continued in the interior. The perception of light, the changes it undergoes in time and space, its shades and variety, its refinement and intensity become the actual experience in Bregenz – but not when it is being observed in terms of external things. Richard Meier is also concerned to bring light into the rooms in the Getty Center. He arranges the galleries in such a way that we are constantly taken past glass surfaces that admit the daylight. And in the galleries themselves the high, pyramidal ceilings in the centre show a square of blue sky that is shaded with slats if the light is too bright. Peter Zumthor keeps this unrefracted natural light outside. He cleans it of all the accidental features to which it is prone. There is no sky, no roof, no tree, no water to be seen. Light is shown as a pure quality, as an absolute, as an abstraction. Double refraction through the outer glass skin and the suspended, etched glass ceiling admits light in its natural tone, but filtered. The slices of space, piled on top of another, are so identical that it is possible to lose one's sense of direction. Everything has an almost three-dimensional presence, right down to the latch on the door, and refers to nothing. Only the light provides a sense of direction. As a visitor, one follows a highly symbolic path up towards the light. The higher you climb up the building, the further you are away from the ground, as the height of the clerestories over the exhibition galleries changes, the lighter it becomes.

Peter Zumthor's glazed Kunsthaus in Bregenz and the office and restaurant building in black form an urban square.

The art shown here has to measure up to this. It can do this only by finding an abstract form. Because here, at first, in a reversal of the usual process, it becomes something concrete in an abstract space. For his opening exhibition in Bregenz, James Turrell changed the outside of the glass cube into a coloured light installation and put up white three-dimensional bodies in the interior of the halls. Per Kirkeby's large-scale paintings brought the changed light-moods in the paint to life, and he presented his bronzes in strict geometrical formations.

The private museum for the Goetz Collection in Munich by Herzog & de Meuron is one of the earliest examples of minimalist museum architecture.

Louis I. Kahn's design for the Kimbell Art Museum in Forth Worth embeds the museum in a landscaped park with pools of water.

But as soon as many positions were shown in one hall in a group exhibition, the abstract quality of the space destroyed the effect of the individual works.

The Kunsthaus in Bregenz is the most extreme manifestation of the "white cube" concept, even if floor and walls remain concrete-grey, which painters like Kirkeby approve of because of the favourable reflection of light. The building demonstrates a position of radical irreconcilability: in this gentle light, art cannot allow itself any attacks of worldly weakness, and no ordinary day can find anything in common with it. The museum insists upon an aesthetic space as a place for "the other", that cannot be made any part of economy, nature, tourism, restaurant etc. There is no view of Lake Constance. The galleries are closed containers, the roof with its magnificent view of mountains and the bay is closed. The bar, like the shop and the offices are outside the museum in their own, black-designed building.

The extreme position of the Bregenz building also becomes clear when another recent design by Swiss architects is recalled. Herzog & de Meuron's museum for the Goetz Collection is considered an early icon of exhibition vessels reduced to absolute essentials. Interestingly, the Basel architects now also distance themselves from their Munich showpiece. They do not see the private museum as a prototype for art museums today, and point out that its features are derived exclusively from their brief: the maximum building height permitted by the municipal building regulations made it necessary to build down into the ground if the necessary volume was to be created. Using lateral toplighting to create two identical light situations made it possible to make visitors forget that they were in a cellar. Herzog & de Meuron do not think that this idea would work for larger building volumes. Reduction to a minimum becomes a question of scale. Be that as it may, with the arrival of AIDS at the latest, time and death came up from the subcutaneous plane and back on to the everyday agenda of contemporary art. And with them there is access to museums for everything that was kept out of the "white cube" time vacuum. And first of all this means external nature. It is no longer the opponent that has to be kept out of art's artificial space in order to protect the utopias of Modernism, in order to collect energy to master nature, to conquer her unpredictabilities and coincidences and to make life more accountable, as an artist like Mondrian wished to do. Modern art always turned in waves to society's pictorial world, to the city as a living-space. Long after the start of the ecological crisis and awareness of a crisis of technological progress it opened up to nature. And the museum went along with it. Even the Galerie Goetz is presented as part of a park. Trees and sky are reflected in the glass bands, so that the borders between them are almost dissolved visually. Birches have not just moved close up to the museum, the wooden wall surfaces are also made of birch-wood.

The Kirchner Museum in Davos by Annette Gigon and Mike Guyer is linked with the landscape by its various outlooks.

This dialogue with nature has its tradition. Following in the footsteps of middle-class villas, the New York Metropolitan Museum of Art is situated in a park. Central Park can be used as an approach space. Louis Kahn prepared visitors to the Kimbell Art Museum in Fort Worth for the experience of art in a similar way, with parks and pools of water. Nature is used as a device for purifying the senses and bringing psyche and spirit into harmony. Architects have taken up links of this kind again in the past few years. For their Kirchner Museum in Davos, Annette Gigon and Mike Guyer have created closed exhibition spaces (with one exception) that are entirely in the tradition of the "white cube". But between the un-hierarchically arranged exhibition containers they open up the building with high windows facing in various directions, looking out over the dramatic world of the Davos mountains that Kirchner repeatedly painted in the second half of his creative life. In his museum for the Fondation Beyeler in Riehen, Renzo Piano strengthens these links even more. The 120 m long pavilion is fitted in between the two border walls in a mature park on the periphery of Basel, and grows out of the ground with its red stone cladding. The roof has many layers, and allows the daylight moods to flow in. A long conservatory invites visitors to rest while looking at the panorama of the adjacent fields. But even more than in Davos or the Kimbell Art Museum the landscape is related directly to the art. A pool with water-lilies comes right up to the three exhibitions galleries, which are glazed at the front. The reflected light from the pool flickers over the white walls and becomes a counterpart to Monet's great landscape of water-lilies on the opposite wall. The real pool and Monet's colour inspiration are both in the viewer's field of vision at the same time. In the case of Alberto Giacometti's sculptures, nature outlines the setting for the figures behind the glass as a social, artistic space for the gaze, and this space is not merely changed by the moods of the day but has to hold its own against nature first of all. Other museums hold nature at arm's length as a medium for rest and recreation, and art then has to measure itself against its magnificent vistas: in the case of the Moderna Museet in Stockholm it is the view of the sea from the restaurant, in Frank O. Gehry's Guggenheim Museum in Bilbao the cascading glass foyer in front of the river, in Richard Meier's Getty Center it is the commanding feeling above the city-plain of Los Angeles and the many glazed walkways and terraces that invite visitors to move from outside to inside and back again.

Alberto Giacometti's sculptures have to hold their own against the landscape setting in Renzo Piano's museum for the Beyeler Collection in Riehen near Basel.

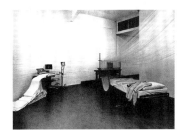

The living world penetrates the museum: the American artist Janine Antoni sleeps in the museum and weaves her sleep-rhythms into a blanket during the day.

Frank O. Gehry was one of the first artists to use an early factory hall, for his "Temporary Contemporary" in Los Angeles, 1983.

The museum as workplace: the German media artist Thom Barth built a cube of offset foils in Stuttgart and got students to work on it.

Jean Nouvel brings three buildings together under one roof in his Culture and Congress Centre in Lucerne and opens them on to Lake Lucerne.

The social world also penetrates museums in the nineties. Here it is not just "art as a commercial system" that comes under scrutiny, or that the strategies used by artists for intervening in society are recorded in objects, drawings or photographs. The museum itself is turned into a location for life. In 1994 the American artist Janine Antoni moved a loom and a bed into the Kunsthaus in Zurich. At night she recorded her REM values with a somnograph, and during the day she wove these sleep patterns into a blanket that kept her warm at nights in its turn. Such works are linked to Vito Acconci's masturbating in a gallery and to Joseph Beuys's living with a coyote, but young artists do not let their actions become rituals. For example, Douglas Gordon set up corner seating in exhibitions in which magazines, books, CDs and video-cassettes, and also drinks, invited visitors to avail themselves of information and have a chat. The Viennese artist Gerwald Rockenschaub always plays records in art venues like a DJ. Rirkrit Tiravanija cooks in the museum and makes musical instruments available. Art is a feast, the museum is its party-pad. But not just that.

Work too seizes this institution that actually, on the basis of Kantian aesthetics, legitimizes itself in middle-class society by eliminating the constraints of functional and rational usability. But the more industrial production and the everyday self-staging of mercantile appearance want something special that makes them distinct from their surroundings, the more art preserves the unassuming quality of everyday things, right down to the packaging material. Marcel Duchamp's concept of the readymade was the model for this, the media-world of pop provided images, the locations of the world of work, industrial halls, warehouses and lofts, provided studios for artists, and exhibition venues as well, later on. Frank O. Gehry's 1983 work "Temporary Contemporary" in Los Angeles is an early example of the change of use undergone by industrial spaces, which quickly became fashionable. The halls for recent art in Schaffhausen and Donald Judd's museum in Marfa, Texas created what are probably the most coherent links between the new ambience and (mainly Minimalist) art. Joseph Beuys had already logically made the museum into a power-station with his sheet-copper installations. And recently the trend swung back to classical Modernism: Renzo Piano copied Brancusi's studio as a museum for the Centre Georges Pompidou in Paris. The Californian artist Jason Rhoades, for example, shows how close the links are to contemporary art here; he sometimes calls his car his studio and has shown his respect for Brancusi's studio by using utensils from the DIY store. But it did not stop at the objects and spaces. Very recently, artists started to take the working process itself into the museum. We have already mentioned Janine Antoni. Richard Serra's gigantic curved-steel sculpture "Snake" was welded together in the great hall of the Guggenheim in Bilbao, and the space, the size of a football pitch, became a factory hall. The German media artist Thom Barth recently went a step further in the domed hall of the Württembergischer Kunstverein in Stuttgart when he set up a giant cube made up of offset film with pictorial material from all over the world on desks and encouraged art students to work on it. The material they produced was exhibited on the walls of the cube. And so there were still art objects in the traditional sense. But work as a process and life-form became the actual object of the exhibition; in the world of life outside the doors of the museum this is becoming rarer and rarer, and is thus a social distinction.

Contemporary art in the nineties draws its energy from bringing areas that were previously separate into contact with each other, and the museums are doing it as well. "Learning from Las Vegas", Robert Venturi's idea of mixing high and low, understanding chaos as a form of order, is one of the planning requirements for some new museum buildings. The museum is seen as a public place that has to offer all the qualities that attract contemporaries and make them want to linger. Jean Novel, the fervent urban development chaos artist among contemporary architects, has not yet built a museum, but a series of cultural centres. In Lucerne he is combining congress centre, concert hall and art gallery, and opening them up to the lake with a restaurant, water, terraces and a large entrance hall. Richard Meier has laid out the Getty Center with its seven institutions as a village or campus, in which even the museum is made up of several pavilions. It is not just that visitors are constantly led though the exterior space, via steps, squares or a garden, not only that the view opens up to the Santa Monica mountains, the Los Angeles urban landscape and the sea on all sides. Inside the individual museum pavilions as well the public space of corridors, stairs, transverse links and walkways take up just as much space as the exhibition galleries. Frank O. Gehry has surrounded the Guggenheim in Bilbao with steps and ramps, which link it with both the town and the river-bank and give the river, which was formerly isolated as an industrial zone, back to the town for the first time. Herzog & de Meuron take this urban element inside the building: the inside of the new Tate Gallery is presented as an art forum of almost antique dimensions. The gigantic machine hall of the old power-station was dug out to ground level so that its full height can be experienced. Under the roof are exhibition areas for sculpture, a lecture hall, cafeteria and access to the exhibition galleries on either side. The museum is staged as a roofed urban space, like the 19th-century Parisian arcades. And Rafael Moneo's double museum on the Stockholm island of Skeppsholmen itself becomes a great cross-reference to the city.

Richard Meier placed the Getty Center as a campus on a hill above Los Angeles.

Opening up urban space also has a considerable effect on the traditional function of the museum. It remains a canonical location. The more art moves closer to the everyday, the more it needs the museum's defining power that identifies it as art with the freedoms of art. Marcel Duchamp ironized this succinctly at an early stage: in his "Boîte-en-Valise" his works were collected symbolically as miniature replicas and copies, and the museum was defined as a sample-case. The museum also remains a place of memory, the cultural community's source of identity, even when that community is globally organized. Although its character does acquire an industrial aspect: it has become a warehouse, a store for materials, goods and means of production that are deployed for maximum profit in the art business. Renzo Piano constructed a storage container on the roof of the Menil Collection in Houston that works like a theatrical properties department for art. But no contemporary artist shaped this new memory status as early and succinctly as the three-dimensional artist Franz Erhard Walther with his so-called "1. Werksatz" (First Work-Set; 1963–1969). 58 forms, mostly made of fabric, are packed into a rectangle and wait to be used in an active piece of work that the artist carries out in a precise sequence. The things that can be seen rolled and piled up here are not, however interesting they may be formally, an actual work, but only a "work-piece", a tool, like the saw and the hammer that are used to manufacture an object.

Herzog & de Meuron are designing a gigantic inner-city hall in a disused London power station for the new Tate Gallery building.

Renzo Piano placed a storage container for paintings on the roof of the Menil Collection in Houston.

The German artist Franz Erhard Walther designed the Kunsthalle Ritter in Klagenfurt.

The Viennese artist Franz West designed benches in the open air for documenta IX in 1992.

How can the museum fulfil both functions? How can it be an institution that sets standards, that raises people above their everyday lives and yet is also open to everyday things? How can museum architecture react to the fact that some artists express themselves architecturally? Not just by coming up with their own designs for museum buildings, as in the case of Erwin Heerich with the Museum Island Hombroich, Donald Judd in Marfa, Ulrich Rückriem in Clonegal in Ireland or Franz Erhard Walther with the Ritter art gallery in Klagenfurt, to name but a few. Gerwald Rockenschaub has been changing exhibition venues for years by installing walls or other structural interventions. Franz West is much in demand as a seating designer. Vito Acconci contributed a library design to documenta X. The more precisely art adapts itself to the everyday, the more artists make it into a strategy within their world, the more often they intervene in museums themselves, the more autonomous and sometimes the more sculptural the architects' museum buildings become. Frank Lloyd Wright's Guggenheim rotunda in New York, already an icon of dysfunctional museum architecture, made a stand in this way. Abstract Expressionist artists had almost made the walls and spaces disappear with their pictures, and all but made the picture itself into a space into which smaller viewers could almost physically step, whereas Wright bent the wall and made it assert itself again as an autonomous element of museum space architecture. Conversely, Frank O. Gehry now claims the freedom of art for his architecture. His strategy makes his buildings into sculptures, which enjoy the protection and perception of art.

In the most recent museum buildings the return of chronology has made the whole range of spatial design possible. The Getty Center is full of historically slanted spaces for its decorative art collections. The pictures hang on fabric, or at least on brightly-painted walls. And small sculptures stand in a little room two storeys high that quotes the breadth of Renaissance sculpture halls. But existing museums as well are increasingly introducing a historical element into their galleries. The Impressionist galleries in the Metropolitan Museum of Modern Art in New York have recently acquired fluted columns. The National Gallery in London has been decorated with plush and English furniture. False ceilings are being removed from many buildings, enfilades reopened, the old spatial intentions restored. Even historically sceptical Modernism, with its bright, white cells is becoming historical, quotable and thus able to be used for specific purposes. Herzog & de Meuron are making suitable spaces for classical art available in the new Tate Gallery in London, and at the same time leaving the rooms in their rough state in the former oil stores. Thus work and space can come into contact in various ways.

Renzo Piano created the purest possible accord for the masterworks of modern harmony in the Fondation Beyeler. It is as though the architect and his client wanted to whisper to the visitors: relax, don't be upset. There is still a *Gesamtkunstwerk* made up of the building and of art. Art does not have to be protected. It is simply there, as a *hortus conclusus*, as a place of joy. It is a guaranteed residue of harmony. Piano said that the aims of his design were "calme, luxe et volupté". His Basel museum has a perfection that is no longer imbued with desire. No loud sound and no cold breath can get inside. Art is still warming fire, time standing still, that interrupts nothing and never passes. In his design for a

Frank Lloyd Wright's spiral for the Solomon R. Guggenheim Museum in New York is an icon of non-functional museum architecture.

double museum of modern art and architecture in Stockholm, Rafael Moneo has not actually played with the chaos that also determines art either. The walls outside the exhibition galleries are clad in wood, the floors are parquet, and the rooms follow a square basic unit of six metres per side, which play around and emphasize the pattern on the parquet and the ceilings, which rise in the shape of pyramids. Nothing seems left to chance. Even the labyrinthine sequence of spaces is so precisely calculated that it confuses visitors only so much that they perceive the austere geometry as making sense. Art, the architect seems to be saying, is calculation. The architect has to confront it with a different kind of calculation. This does not work for many contemporary artists. They do not necessarily want to have to do with squares when placing their sculptures, installations and videos. Moneo points out that he actually designed the majority of the galleries for the Moderna Museet's collection as well. And that is famous for show-pieces of classical Modernism, for its works by Duchamp, Léger, Picasso, Breton, Magritte, Tatlin and many others, rather like the Beyeler Museum in Riehen. But Frank O. Gehry issues a challenge to contemporary artists. The expressively plunging foyer is a hyperbole of Frank Lloyd Wright's New York rotunda. Galleries and spatial sequences branch off from it in three directions, some are classical in shape, some curve, taper at the top, and are broken by walkways and balconies. Only works that can respond to this, usually commissioned, like Jenny Holzer's LCD installation, can hold their own. The architecture wins the day against many other works: James Rosenquist's pictures, up to seven metres wide, Claes Oldenburg's monumental "Knife Ship", a cross between a tank and a Swiss army knife, even Richard Serra's specially prepared steel shells for his sculpture "Snake", 31 metres long, shrink to the scale of toys in the 130 m long hall.

Renzo Piano's building for the Fondation Beyeler, from the outside.

But almost more important to the architects than the exhibition rooms are links with the surrounding area, which turn a building into a place. In Lucerne, Jean

Nouvel provides a centre for the area between the station and the post office, and opens it up to the old town opposite, on the other side of the river and the lake. The large flat roof, covering all three buildings, and the play with the light reflected on the water, relate over and above this to the lake and the mountains. Herzog & de Meuron's suggestion for the extension at the New York Museum of Modern Art pulls large sections of the heterogeneous building complex together with a crystalline glass skin, which mediates with the glass and stones façades of Manhattan. A tower that turns from street to street and thus overlooks the whole site makes the museum an identifiable landmark amid the many skyscrapers. And Rafael Moneo drew the whole form of his double museum from consideration of the existing building stock at the location. He chose the Swedish Navy's old parade hall on the island of Skeppsholmen as his starting-point; this had previously been occupied by the art gallery, and he built the new museum on to this, linked it with the new architecture museum on the other side of the old hall and hid the complex behind the existing buildings. The entrance is a modest portico. Anyone coming up the hill sees only a few figures by Jean Tinguely and Niki de Saint Phalle. The museum cowers away in need of protection. On the sea side it is placed on the slope like a castle that permits no one to look inside. Only the large glazed façade of the restaurant gives an open view of the sea and the promenade opposite. Art, the building seems to be saying, needs seclusion, it needs a protected space, otherwise it cannot develop its energy and project it into society. Characteristically the new museum that does its utmost not to be a landmark is most visible at night. Lighting cubes shine out above the bazaar-like conglomerate of exhibitions galleries. The light defines the spaces, and it shines out into the city. The museum as a place of light.

These buildings offer the particular society that has commissioned them a whole package of possible experiences. They make it possible for people to find images of their own experience that can be zapped in between the café and the

Herzog & de Meuron suggested making the Museum of Modern Art in New York into a landmark by designing an unconventional tower.

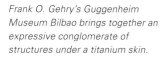

Frank O. Gehry's Guggenheim Museum Bilbao brings together an expressive conglomerate of structures under a titanium skin.

sea-view and nevertheless penetrate so far beyond the flood of images that they stick. They are, and in this entirely compensation phenomena in the social sensual system, public places in a private age, in which, alongside the big stories that have become questionable, many small ones are possible as well, starting and breaking off in a most complex fashion. Thus they become, regardless of the medium chosen by the artist, locations of a time that has become fragmented and enlivened, time rediscovered.

Rafael Moneo almost hides the long Moderna Museet complex in Stockholm behind existing buildings.

The Museum as Sculpture

Interview with Frank O. Gehry on the Guggenheim Museum Bilbao

What problems have contemporary concepts of art museums for an architect today?

Frank O. Gehry

The biggest problem is that there is no consensus on what a museum is and what the needs of a museum are. Except that there is a very strong mythology accepted by most architects: that a museum for art has to be differential and neutral in order that it does not compete with the art. And that mythology is repeated like a mandala. Every architect I hear starts out talking about this neutrality and they all build museums that try to be neutral but actually fail in their neutrality, because they do not know how to do it. Some of the architects detail to death the walls, the lights, the skylights, the floors and the doors. They make so much an overpowering detail fetish out of the architecture in search for neutrality that those details become overpowering to some art, although not to everything. The classic example for me, and this is attacking the holy land, is the Kimbell Museum in Dallas. Even though from the outside and conceptually it is one of Kahn's best buildings, it is difficult on the art, because of this relentless detailing which Kahn didn't do in many other buildings. The artists would rather be in a very strong building. They do not want to be in a neutral box. I have heard it many times over the years: Oh god, another neutral gallery, stupid.

Who told you this?

Daniel Buren for example has been very much on my case about that for twenty years now. Or Michael Asher. And recently I have heard it from artists that are in Bilbao. Julian Schnabel feels that the kind of architecture that I made excited him to play with. I got the same from Jim Dine, from Francesco Clemente. Rauschenberg said to me at the opening of Bilbao that, when he was asked, won't this architecture compete with your art, he said, I will make better art. I think the artists need and want a kind of partnership. Art looks different in different places and context is a big deal. If you put a Breughel in a garage it looks different than if you put it into the Kunsthistorisches Museum in Vienna. Eventually the painting is the painting and you overcome context and you look at the painting, but it seems to me that you can help the work.

What do you feel about Richard Serra's "Snake"? From the balcony of the gallery the huge sculpture looks incredibly small.

I had a very big difference of opinion with how that gallery was to be used. I had always seen it with walls in it so that when you were in the rooms the skylights were so high up they were not in your eye. Now when you look up the skylight is too busy for the art. I never intended it to be that way. But my client, Guggenheim Foundation Director Thomas Krens, likes the big open spaces. You can talk to him about it.

Frank O. Gehry built the surrounding area with its motorway bridge, railway line and river bank into his design for the Guggenheim Museum. The museum creature pushes its tail under the bridge. The building mediates between the river and the higher part of the city.

The lid covering the railway line serves as a piazza linking the museum with the city quarter.

The final model of the museum followed many predecessors.

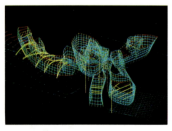

Catia computer studies of the museum made precise calculations possible.

What about the other galleries?

All the other spaces are okay. The two other galleries on the ground floor are storage rooms that we converted for temporary use as gallery. I think they are not hung properly as well. There is too much stuff in them. But I am very pleased with how they hung the classical galleries. I think the LeWitt is not his best piece and he agrees. He wants to go back and redo it.

What about performance and video art?

In the long gallery and in the shaped galleries I used catwalks. The intention was that they could use it for performance art. Those galleries could be used for theatrical pieces. You could put follow spots and do all kinds of things from the catwalks. Originally they were intended to be electrically operated so that you could bring them down to the floor and bring them up again. But they did not put the money into that.

One of your early works was the Temporary Contemporary in Los Angeles, which is rather an industrial space.

I did not do anything in there. I swept the floor.

In that case it was part of the concept to restrict yourself. How did you develop from there to doing a museum building like a sculpture?

I always had that point of view from the time when I used to argue with Buren twenty years ago and he used to get mad at me when I talked about neutral buildings. Many artists used to argue with me. And they would say: Frank, don't you understand, we want to be at an important place. So your building has to be important in the community. If it is not equal to a city's courthouse and the library and the concert hall, it is second rate. That's the point.

The building can have an iconic presence, can be important and it does not trivialize the art. In fact it enhances it.

Your building is a sculpture, a piece of art itself. Is this a strategy of architecture to survive today?

There is no strategy. I have evolved since 1962, when I started to practise. You can see the evolution of my work. Architecture has to have emotion and feeling. I got interested in movement instead of decoration. It is just one person's take on it. In fact most architecture follows a trend to get back to minimalism. It is sort of a pseudominimalist world that the younger people in Europe are doing, which I find discouraging. It is very cold and in its own way decorative. It is using minimalism in a decorative way.

Your building often is compared to Frank Lloyd Wright's Guggenheim building in New York. Did you have Wright's rotunda in mind?

No. I never thought the rotunda worked for art. I have seen many shows there. And the only ones I ever liked were the Flavin or Oldenburg or Calder, when there were three-dimensional objects. I never liked the painting shows. But I was told by the curator Diane Waldman who has been there for twenty-five years that I was wrong, that the artists really loved the provocation. And that is what Thomas Krens pushed me to do. He wanted that kind of provocation in Bilbao. My first designs for the atrium in Bilbao were very neutral.

The museum under construction.

Building site and surrounding area.

The titanium skin changes its expression and colour with the light and produces edges that can be bizarre (detail).

They were very much like a marble quarry with big shelves and blocks so you could hang paintings on it. Tom hated them. He said, that is too neutral.

The atrium is very expressive. How much are you related to German Expressionism?

I don't know. I look at a lot of stuff. That could easily come from Hieronymus Bosch as it came from German Expressionism or from Brancusi or Matisse's cut-outs. I am like a vacuum cleaner. I go to museums and look at paintings. It is the thing I do most in life.

You take your buildings apart like deconstructing the whole and they keep together like figures nevertheless.

I love watching people at a cocktail party and the different clothes and the different expressions. And you see it in paintings. The greatest painting of all for that is "Las Meniñas" by Francisco Goya where all the action is going on between all the players. It's got emotion in it. I want to put emotion in my architecture.

Is that why you use figures like mother and child in your architecture, why you make the building like being a body?

I guess there is some of that. I am fascinated with mother and child, because it is so basic. And I am sure it is a built-in value that inspires some kind of emotion. As well the fold: When you are born and you lie in your mother's arm the first thing you touch are the folds of her clothes. In our time movement creates emotion. I have been trying to use that. Since Bilbao I have got it more fluid.

A high, curved exhibition gallery with large pictures by Anselm Kiefer.

What is the relation to the old value of *firmitas*? Is it in contrast with today's world and architecture?

Last year Vittorio Lampugnani arranged a conference on firmitas at the ETH Zurich. I think he was hoping to have a discussion about stone and I came in with a third of a millimetre of titanium that has more firmitas than stone, because it has a hundred year guarantee not to change anything. Whereas stone deteriorates in the modern world. What is firmitas today? What is really the value of it, too? Our culture has always felt the buildings had to be made to last. But in fact many buildings that were made to last have already been torn down in the spirit of progress. So what is the force that is creating our environment? Çertainly it is not the architect. It is an economic power and a political power.

Even large works of art look tiny in the large exhibition gallery, which is 130 m long.

A traditional cubic exhibition gallery for Classical Modernism.

What do you want to achieve with a building in a city say like Bilbao?

I wanted the Guggenheim Bilbao to have an iconic presence in the city. I wanted it to work for the arts. I wanted it to connect to the city, to the bridge, to the water, to the 19th century, so that it became a usable part of the city in the same spirit that Hans Hollein made the Städtische Museum Abteiberg in Mönchengladbach in its relation to the church and to the small town, in the same spirit as James Stirling's Stuttgart museum did to climbing the hill from the lower street to the higher street to the music school. That is the spirit of urbanism I tend to be interested in.

Coming back to museums and yet another aspect of *firmitas*: How was the construction of the Guggenheim Museum Bilbao done?

I used the curtain wall system. The structure under there is a very unique one. There is a steel structure that is conceived as a basket. Where the building bulges out and becomes convex the structure as a basket is much more efficient for wind and we were able to save money on the steel by doing that. The steel prices came in eighteen per cent under budget. Some

View into the 50 m high atrium with
its tumbling cascades of glass.

The expressive forms of the atrium
are reminiscent of Fritz Lang's film
"Metropolis".

of those moves are really practical. Nobody talks about them that way because that
wasn't the paramount thing.

How did you chose titanium for the surface?

It took two years. Originally I wanted
to use lead copper. But lead copper is outlawed now in most countries. Aluminum
does not maintain its colour and it is vulnerable to pollution. Zinc goes black and I didn't
like that. Then you have stainless steel. We made a panel that had fifty examples of
variety. We looked at it in the light in Bilbao, but I didn't like it. By accident I found a
piece of titanium. I put it on the wall outside my office in Santa Monica and it rained
that day. And the small piece turned gold in colour in the rain. I went crazy. We got
bigger sheets of it, but none of them looked like my sample. We spent a year trying
to get the surface back to look like it. And we made it half the thickness of stainless
steel and could still get the guarantee of firmitas. It was papery and it would make the
building look very fragile. One of its greatest attributes is how it plays with the light in
that part of the country.

How did you choose the site? It is one of the ugliest sites one could imagine.

I loved it. I like the bridge. I like the idea of connecting to the bridge. That comes from Fritz Lang images. That comes from the S-Bahn going through between the Bode and the Pergamon Museum in Berlin. Those images of modernity, of movement in cars and trains and planes in relation to buildings that Fritz Lang and others gave, portray ideal architecture for the twentieth century. The visionary stuff interested me and I like all these collisive things that were happening with the city at that point. I did not

*The museum is edged by a broad pool of water
on the river-bank side. A gigantic baldacchino covers
the terrace in front of the atrium.*

only pick the site myself though. Guggenheim Director Thomas Krens did, too. We picked it separately without knowing from each other.

Would you say Bilbao is a museum for the next century?

A lot of people think it is. It was certainly designed with that in mind and it was based on collections that the Guggenheim is interested in. But nobody can foresee the future. The perverse world may very well decide that small boutique museums are the thing of the future. If you look at the Panza Collection, which the Guggenheim acquired and the collections of sculpture and painting that were collected in the last thirty years there are very few museums in the world that can do this. The Tate Gallery in London is obviously trying to do something like that. Obviously the Museum of Modern Art in New York has a different agenda. That is the nice thing about democracy. It does not have to be only one way.

Ground floor plan.

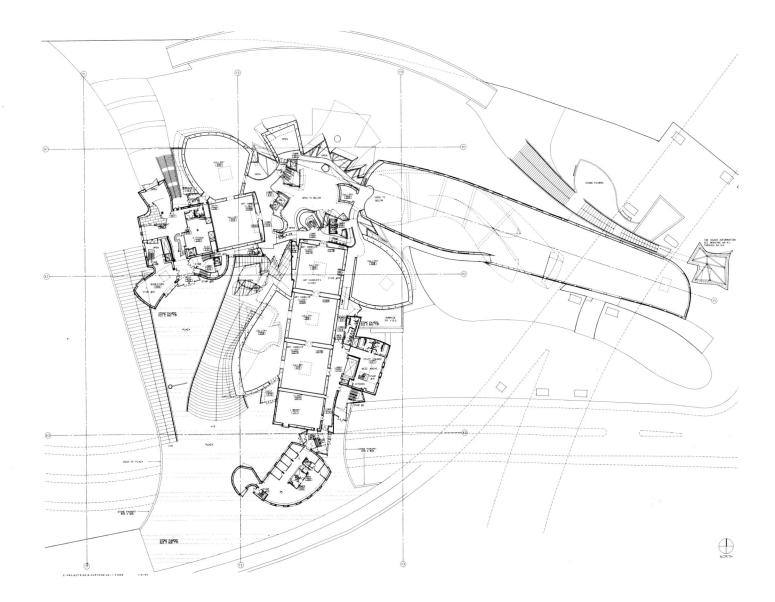

Longitudinal section.

Cross-section.

River side elevation.

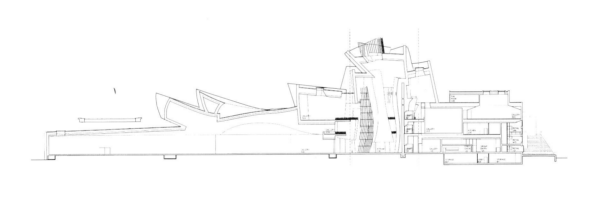

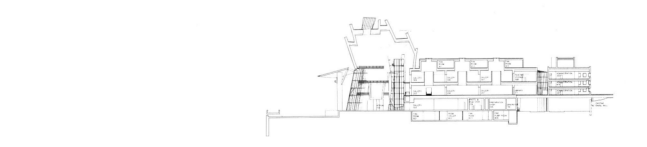

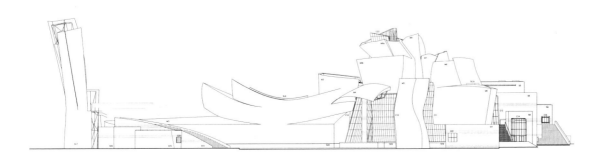

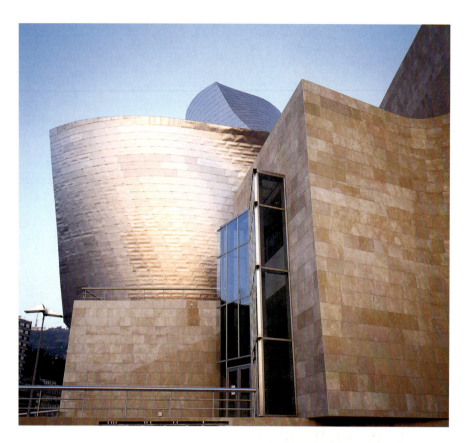

Stone, glass and sheet titanium are starkly juxtaposed.

The foyer opens on to pool and river under a large baldacchino.

The curved building has a lot of empty corners inside.

Classical exhibition gallery showing contemporary Spanish art.

View into the foyer.

New Museum

Frank O. Gehry and the New York Solomon R. Guggenheim Foundation have chosen one of the most awkward sites in the former industrial city for the Guggenheim Museum in Bilbao. The broad curve of the river Nervion cuts the city into two halves. A multi-laned motorway bridge crosses the valley. A railway line leads to the former industrial and port facilities by the river. The new town is set higher, and has no access to the river-banks. Gehry's design integrates all these unmanageable elements with a triumphantly exploding sculptural building between the new town and the river. The building grows up in fissured volumes from a travertine base, thrusts through under the motorway bridge and embraces it with a signaltower whose steel scaffolding and stone slabs are left deconstructively bare. The angles, edges, sloping surfaces and soft curves of the building are covered with a titanium skin that reacts to every change in the light and makes the museum into a gleaming foreign body that defines the town. A rectangular travertine block and an oval volume respond to the new town. They support a large piazza that covers the railway line and leads down to the museum entrance, which is placed lower. A large ramp with steps provides access to the river-bank. A pool surrounding the museum forms a transition to the river. In the interior, the 50 m high atrium with its plunging glass cascades, rising supports and floating walkways dizzies the eye. This expressive architectural gesture offers art different spaces in three wings branching off the atrium. A hall 130 m long and 30 m wide shrinks giant sculptures by Claes Oldenburg and Richard Serra to miniatures. Curved spaces and angular corners are sound when artists have conceived work for them. Subtle painting, like Minimal Art, for example, has problems with the difficult lighting conditions. Most convincing are the classically tailored rooms for Modern art. The architecture is more of an experience than the art in the Guggenheim Museum Bilbao. The building offers the Guggenheim art empire a chance to show some of its more unwieldy works.

Location
Abandoibarra Etorbidea 2
48001 Bilbao, Spain,
telephone: + 34 94 423 27 88

Client
Basque Country Government

Competition
1991

Construction
1993–1997

Architects
Frank O. Gehry & Associates, Santa Monica

Main project team
Frank O. Gehry (chief architect), Randy Jefferson (project director), Vano Haritunians (project manager), Douglas Hanson (project architect), Edwin Chan (project designer)

Other members of the team
Rich Barrett, Tomaso Bradshaw, Karl Blette, Matt Fineout, Bob Hale, David Hardie, Michael Hootman, Grzegotz Kosmal, Naomi Langer, Mehran Mashayekh, Chris Mercier, Brent Miller, David Reddy, Marc Salette, Bruce Shepard, Rick Smith, Eva Sobesky, Derek Soltes, Todd Spiegel, Jeff Wauer, Kristin Woehl

Executing architects and engineers
IDOM, Bilbao
José Maria Asumendi (project director), Luis Rodriguez Llopis (project manager), César Caicoya (architect responsible)

Structural engineers
Skidmore, Owings & Merrill, Chicago

Mechanical engineering
Cosentini Associates, New York

Lighting technology
Lam Partners, Boston

Security
Roberto Bergamo E. A.

Acoustic and audio-visual systems
Mc Kay, Connant, Brook, Inc., Los Angeles

Theatre experts
Peter George Associates, New York

Contractors
Cimentaciones Abando (foundations)
Ferrovial, Lauki, Urssa (steel & concrete structure)
Construcciones y Promociones Balzola (external building)
Ferrovial (interiors, building systems, site works)

Gross floor area
24,290 m^2

Exhibition area
10,560 m^2

Building costs
100 million US-$

Bibliography
Coosje van Bruggen,
Frank O. Gehry Guggenheim Museum Bilbao, New York/Stuttgart 1997.
Frank Gehry 1991–1995,
El Croquis 74/75, Madrid 1995.

Site plan.

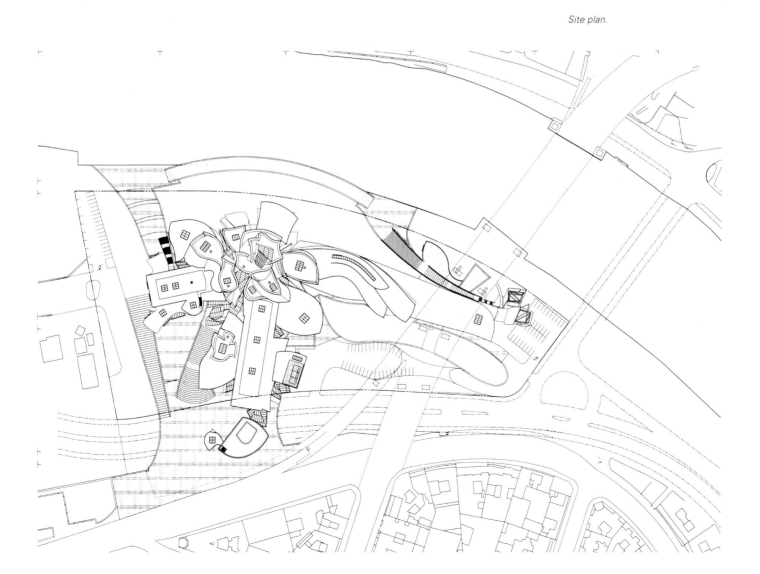

The Museum as Urban Space

Interview with Jacques Herzog on the projects for the Museum of Modern Art, New York, and the Tate Gallery of Modern Art, London

You gave the project for the Museum of Modern Art, which is now not to be realized, a dedication as a title: "Art and People in the 21st Century". That sounds very personal and programmatic at the same time. What was it all about?

When we design spaces for art we work on the basis that people and art relate to each other. We believe that art will still be very important in the next century. We don't see it as simply one form of entertainment alongside others, but as a possibility for showing people how to approach things and understand them – as Bruce Nauman put it in his video work: "The true artist helps the world by revealing mystic truths."

So how does architecture come into it?

Architecture that builds spaces for this art should stimulate people to come to terms with it. It should help them to perceive this art in the best possible way. It should create important places where people like to linger, and that can mean a lot of people, when I think of the great museums in London and New York. I wanted people to be able to see things in such a way that they can make discoveries and enjoy surprises – so that they carry an experience that will live on in their everyday lives away from the museum with them.

How did you address that in concrete terms for the MoMA project?

The whole project is larded with special places and ideas of this kind. For example, one central place was the sculpture garden. We developed exhibition spaces around it on three sides, and thus made it into the centre of the exhibition area.

*Jacques Herzog
Pierre de Meuron
Christine Binswanger
Harry Gugger*

How did you handle the existing buildings and their individual parts? They embody a certain attitude as well, like the escalator, for example. The competition brief identified reorganizing the interior of the existing building as one of the requirements. Another task was the extension. Did you create hierarchies?

The escalator is inevitable, because so many people use the building. We solved it in such a way that it no longer blocks the view of the garden, as in a department store or the Centre Pompidou in Paris, where it is used as a key design element. We played it down, and shifted steps that need you to put in a physical effort into the foreground. Each wing was given its own, unmistakable staircase. We are doing something similar in the new Tate Gallery. There is a staircase that leads through the entire building. You can then choose how you want to move about. These museums are intended to be heterotopian places in which a number of different qualities can be experienced.

Photo-montage of the Museum of Modern Art with glass façade and tower as an urban landmark, seen from Fifth Avenue and 54th Street.

Computer-generated photo-montage of the north façade with sculpture garden.

How is this breadth expressed in the spatial programme?

MoMA is a conglomerate structure created in various phases. We did not want to homogenize it. We created large coherent areas. But these areas are structured in such a way that the different places in the different buildings remain recognizable. When you move into another part of the building, or in a different direction, large side-windows create links with the garden or the two roads on either side of the building. There are vertical links in the buildings as well. You always know precisely where you are. At the corners and transitions between the different wings there's always a café, a little library, a video room or another place that fulfils a social function and makes the changeover, the joint, into something that you can experience.

What should the interior of the actual exhibition spaces be like?

We kept them in the buildings that were previously used for exhibition purposes, but we changed the proportions of the rooms. At the moment they are too small, too cramped, too low. We have taken out some whole storeys as well.

The conglomerate is held together by a glass skin from the outside. What is its function?

The glass is used in a similar way to other projects in terms of construction: printed or etched glass panes are placed in front of windows or an isolated wall. This creates homogeneity with a progressive transition from transparency to opaqueness, between daylight and artificial light. The glass can also be printed differently, so that sometimes it looks like stone and then again like something that scarcely has a physical presence at all.

Section through the existing Goodwin Stone wing of the Museum of Modern Art.

Section through the west wing and the new north wing.

Longitudinal section parallel with 53rd Street.

Longitudinal section through the sculpture garden.

In urban terms, MoMA has the problem that it is not on an avenue. For this reason it has to be given a particular exterior concision. So you designed a tower that attracts attention less because of its height than because it is an unusual shape.

It is more like a church tower than a high-rise building. This is where the curators work. It is a brain for thinking about and exhibiting art. The tower develops away from the plot in 53rd Street, moves up close to the MoMA high-rise building and looks down past this into the garden. We were more interested in this movement and the change in shape than the height.

What are the implications of this relationship with a church tower? Is that a statement about the social status of today's museums?

No. We don't see it as religious in any way. A museum should be an open and casual place in which the only serious point is that art can show the way ahead socially. The reference to the church tower is about proportions and position in the city. There are some fine examples of small churches in this part of Manhattan that are crammed in between the skyscrapers and yet do not look ridiculous. Our tower wouldn't have looked ridiculous either, because it had its own transparency and crystalline focus. We were very interested in this variety.

East Wing   New Garden Wing

The tower is very firmly an object. Does not architecture that has this kind of object quality immediately enter into a state of tension with the use for which the building is intended, something that causes a lot of curators today to complain that new art museums are in love with themselves and unsuited to exhibiting art?

I think there are enough museums now with simply designed galleries satisfying the need for plainness. But we shall soon see how important it is that architecture should assert itself as architecture. I understand that it seems strange now. We were actually the first to build simple galleries like this, for the Goetz Collection in Munich. But today I should like to differentiate. When we first went to MoMA for the competition there were no visitors and you could see how ugly the galleries were. But that did not matter too much: the works of art outshone all the faults, they asserted their full authority. Of course art is even more attractive if the galleries are better. By this I mean that expressive architecture has its qualities as well. I consider Frank O. Gehry's Guggenheim in Bilbao to be an attractive place. One of the reasons that people are stimulated to go there is because its location is attractive. Then it's perhaps not so important whether the walls are straight or not. I don't simply want to be a good boy and side with the box. The «white box» is not the be all and the end all of showing art. The Tate Gallery in the former Bankside power station will certainly have essentially peaceful galleries. But there will also be a dramatic quality, even though that is not a very good word for our intentions. We want to stretch the senses between large and small spaces. We stage variety, otherwise it's boring.

Model of the new curators' tower with its twisting movement.

The new entrance hall is higher than before and opens up a view of the sculpture garden.

The entrance hall itself becomes an interior continuation of the sculpture garden, as a sculpture hall.

Are you describing a move away from the Goetz gallery?

I am interested in subtle balance. In the case of Goetz it was important that the basement floor was like the upper floor, so that you never got the impression of being underground. But if this museum were five times bigger, you would suddenly wonder whether you are upstairs or downstairs. Then the structure starts to shift, and it's no good any more. It's not possible to give recipes for this.

If you consider the MoMA conglomerate, the new Tate Gallery is the exact opposite. The Bankside building is clearly a powerful figure with a tower almost as high as the dome of St. Paul's Cathedral, which is in sight. What were your first ideas for this building?

In the case of the Tate, this disused power station was simply there. We were the only people in the competition to say: because it is there, we have to address it in such a way that we produce quality. We have left the turbine hall open, indeed we've enlarged it, dug it out, so that we can show as much as possible of the structure. Actually we are exhibiting the building. This decision has far-reaching implications. We could no longer indulge in formal spectacle in the interior, but the internal structure is new. We have used glass almost exclusively for the new galleries. Our language is unambiguous: brick, steel or glass, to reinforce the existing substance.

What fascinated you about this building?

The power station is an important building in urban development terms, placed precisely opposite St. Paul's Cathedral. And it wouldn't be possible to build a new space on the gigantic scale of the turbine hall. Then we were also fascinated simply by the idea of opening the building to the public. It was built to keep them out, like a castle that looks huge from a distance but is inaccessible when you get closer because of the buildings around it. We've turned all that round, pulled down a lot around the outside and opened up the hall with a ramp on the city side. The building becomes a box with glass walls: forbidding and asserting its form, but opening up at the same time. This game of contradictions is an important architectural principle for us. The Tate building offers it on a number of planes. You can go into the great hall and spend time there without coming into contact with the museum. The building has various layers that can be closed off or opened up. The crucial thing will be how the building is used.

Model of an exhibition gallery in the new west wing.

Your most visible exterior intervention is the "light strip" that you have placed on top of the building. How did you arrive at this?

Actually it is a two-storey building in its own right. It gives the Tate its urban character. We related it to the chimney, it reinforces its vertical quality and balances the two elements because of the cross-shape. The light strip is a repository of energy. It contains a restaurant, a great deal of technology and a space that is related to the Goetz gallery because here too light comes in from a height and at the side.

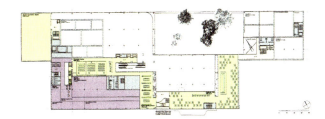

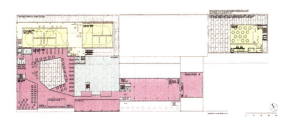

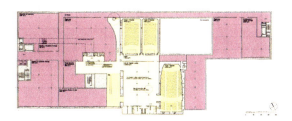

*Ground plans mezzanine, ground floor, theatre level (left) and
4th floor, 3rd floor, 2nd floor (right).*

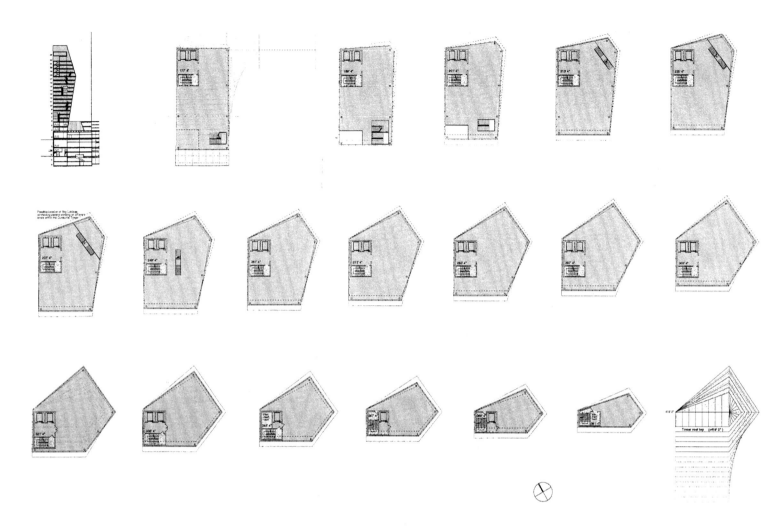

Ground plans of the floors of the new curators' tower from the 6th to the 23rd floor.

What are the key features in the exhibition galleries as far as you are concerned?

We have made the spaces reticent, and given them their own rhythm, spaciousness, height and breadth. Their variety is intended to keep looking at art a continuing pleasure. Visitors should feel that they are moving through different zones. When you go into the turbine hall you have the enormous former boiler house on the left, in which all the museum spaces are packed closely together. At the same time, on the right of the ramp, the way leads to the former oil tanks, into underground spaces for contemporary art, some of which are toplit, but designed less homogeneously in formal terms, and with an open grid that leaves the beams, the electrical cables, the lighting open, as in a loft. In the turbine hall, art is meant to receive the visitors. There are bars in various places. There is a large auditorium in the middle of the building.

As well as these two very large projects, Herzog & de Meuron have designed a large number of exhibition galleries, among other things. What attracts you to the task of designing exhibition spaces for art?

In museums we are fascinated by coming to terms with art and artists, and the fact that they are public buildings. For this reason the Tate is the most interesting project that we have been able to realize so far. It is like a city on a reduced scale.

Extension and Conversion of the Museum of Modern Art

Purchase of the adjacent Dorset Hotel and two other town houses made it possible for the Museum of Modern Art (MoMA) to extend its usable space by 50 per cent, and opens it into the full depth of a street block for the first time. MoMA has used the extension as a chance to design the internal spatial structure more flexibly and lucidly. The brief required that the six departments Painting and Sculpture, Drawings, Prints, Photography, Film and Video, Architecture and Design should all be provided with their own exhibition areas, but that they should be made more permeable to each other, and that the established hierarchies should be broken down. Ten of the younger European, Japanese and American architects' offices were invited, and three of them were asked to provide further detail about their projects in a second round. Herzog & de Meuron responded first of all to the conglomerate of existing museum wings that had been built from 1939 by Philip L. Goodwin & Edward Durrell Stone, Philip Johnson (1951 and 1964) and Cesar Pelli (1984). A large part of the complex is held together by a skin of glass: as the building in the background is not uniform and the glass is compressed in different ways, this produces different levels of transparency and density, which sometimes dissolve the façades in light, but then give them the hardness of stone. This closed appearance is reinforced by a tower, which raises the museum, hidden unassumingly between two avenues, to the status of a landmark. The tower's unusual shape, which was developed from the zoning regulations, sets it into dynamic twisting motion from the plot in 53th Street, past the neighbouring tower by Cesar Pelli and down to the famous sculpture garden in 54rd Street. This movement, and its apparently immaterial glass skin, give the tower, which accommodates the curators' offices, a sovereign and dynamic quality. The exhibition galleries were developed around the central sculpture garden in a new "garden wing" and "north wing", and conceived as large areas permitting the greatest possible freedom of division and use. Windows, reading niches, video rooms, cafeterias and vertical connection mark transitions and make it easier to find one's way in the various sections of the building. The greatly extended entrance hall in the Goodwin & Stone wing is conceived as extending the sculpture garden into the present and signals the character of the place as soon as you walk into it. This design takes a bold look into the future of museum building. This may have been too much for those responsible. Yoshio Taniguchi's winning project restricts itself largely to preserving the existing approaches.

Site plan.

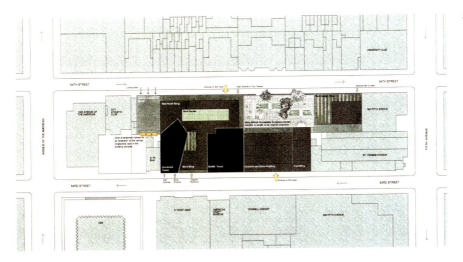

Location
11 West 53 Street, New York, NY 10019, USA, telephone +1 212 708 98 89

Client
Museum of Modern Art, New York

Competition
1997

Architects
Herzog & de Meuron Architekten AG, Basel

Partners in charge
Jacques Herzog, Pierre de Meuron, Harry Gugger, Christine Binswanger

Members of the team
Roland Bachmann, Imre Bartal, Konstanze Beelitz, Bela Berec, Lukas Bögli, Lukas Kupfer, Patrick Linggi, Hansuli Matter, Mario Meier, Reto Oechslin, Koshi Omi, Juan Salgado

Gross floor area
53,883 m², of which 18,580 m² are new space

New exhibition area
12,356 m²

Estimated building costs
Funding campaign for 400 million US$

Bibliography
John Elderfield, Imagining the Future of The Museum of Modern Art. Studies in Modern Art 7, New York 1998.

Converting a Disused Power Station into the New Tate Gallery of Modern Art

The Tate Gallery bought the former Bankside power station so that it could extend its exhibition capacity; the building was designed by Giles Gilbert Scott between 1947 and 1963. The massive brick structure on the Thames is an urban counterpart to St. Paul's Cathedral; its striking central chimney on the façade is almost as high as the cathedral's dome. Despite its tangible physical presence the power station was hemmed in by the surrounding buildings and inaccessible to the public. Herzog & de Meuron took these two features as the starting-point for their design. The surrounding buildings were pulled down, and a park (designed by the landscape architects Kienast Vogel Partner of Zurich and Berne) opens up the bank of the Thames and the area immediately around the building to the public. The monumental quality of the building is emphasized on the outside by a two-storey "light strip" running the whole length of the brick building and adding an immaterial-looking horizontal as the arm of a cross to the chimney, which shoots 118 m up into the sky. Inside, Herzog & de Meuron exploit the full height of the building. The entire interior has been removed, down to the outside walls and the rear layer of the structure, which is still used by the electricity company as a substation. The central turbine hall, which extends over the full length of the building, has been largely excavated so that its full height of 35 m can be used as a hall-like forum. It has entrances at all four points of the compass, and develops its own urban topography, which is also intended to accommodate art exhibitions and film shows. A ramp at the main entrance on the west side will take the anticipated two million visitors per year down into this hall. On the left, in the former boiler-house, are three floors containing 10,000 m^2 of exhibition space, compactly stacked. On the right there is access to spaces with an art gallery atmosphere accommodated in the former oil-tank rooms. The space is designed dynamically: loft-spaces, the spacious foyer and exhibition spaces with a classical look, varied in height, area and lighting, give an intense rhythm to the colossal dimensions. Windows create visual links between the various areas. The detailing addresses the weight of the steel and brick tradition. In the field of materials, concentrating on glass and steel complements the substance of the building, which Herzog & de Meuron are showing with confident reticence.

Location
Bankside Power Station, 25 Sumner Street,
London SE1, England

Client
Tate Gallery, London

Competition
1994

Realization
1995–1999

Architects
Herzog & de Meuron Architekten AG, Basel

Partners in charge
Jacques Herzog, Pierre de Meuron, Harry
Gugger, Christine Binswanger

Project director
Harry Gugger

Members of the team
Thomas Baldauf, Ed Burton, Michael Casey,
Victoria Castro, Peter Cookson, Liam Dewar,
Catherine Fierens, Adam Firth, Matthias
Gnehm, Nik Graber, Konstantin Karagiannis,
Angelika Krestas, Patrik Linggi, José Ojeda
Martos, Filipa Mourao, Yvonne Rudolf, Juan
Salgado, Vicky Thornton, Camilo Zanardini

Construction management
Schal, London

Associate architect
Shepard Robson, London

**Structural engineering, electrical and
sanitary planning, climate control design**
Ove Arup & Partners International, London

Gross floor area
34,547 m^2

Total project costs
£ 130 million

Building costs
£ 41,828,000

Building costs per m^2
£ 1,210

Bibliography
Three volumes planned,
author Rowan Moore.

The former power station was designed in 1947 by Giles Gilbert Scott
as an urban counterpart to St. Paul's Cathedral, which is on the other side
of the Thames.

A disused oil-fired power station on the Thames is being used for the new Bankside Tate Gallery. Herzog & de Meuron express the monumental character of the existing building in their design and at the same time rescind this by placing a band of light rising through several storeys on top of it. This band of light and the high chimney form a cross.

The main entrance at the side leads to the lower-placed ground floor of the building via a long ramp. A pedestrian bridge by Norman Foster connects the new museum to central London on the opposite bank.

View of the original turbine hall with the machinery.

Herzog & de Meuron have the turbine hall completely cleared to let its full height make an impact.

Computer simulation of a high exhibition room.

Computer simulation of the central hall, which can be used for exhibitions and provides access to the exhibition galleries on either side.

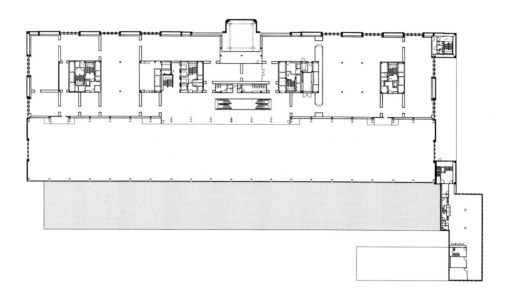

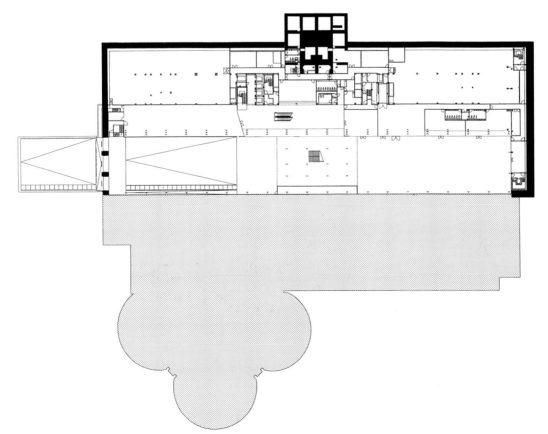

3rd floor.

1st floor.

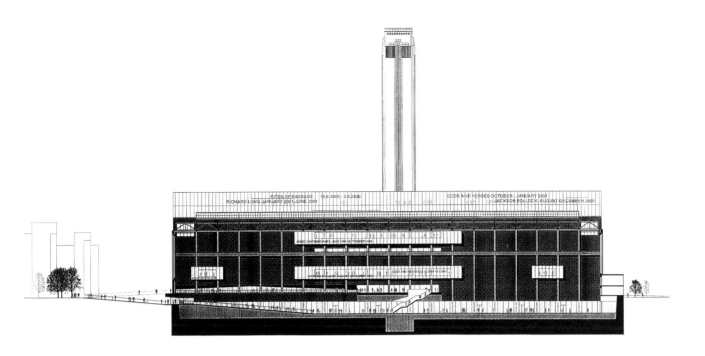

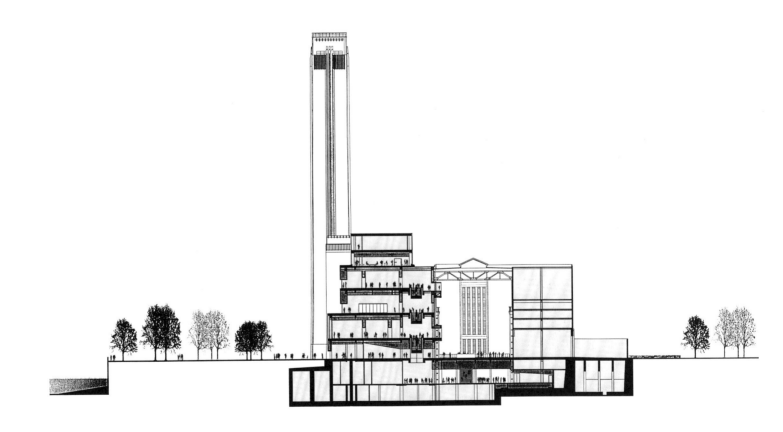

Longitudinal section through the turbine hall.

Cross section through the north entrance.

The Museum as Campus

Interview with Richard Meier on the Getty Center in Los Angeles

Mr Meier, what was your first impression of the site of the Getty Center?

I thought it was fabulous. It was a great hillside in which there was very little vegetation of any character, because the entire site had burnt during the fire that jumped the freeway in 1966. Under the chaparral shrubs a lot of char remained, which meant the site was fairly flexible in terms of what we could do here. There weren't a lot of great trees to be preserved.

Richard Meier

Do you remember your first ideas on the project?

They really came out of the land of the site itself, of the form of the land and the relationship of the land to the city. There are basically two ridges: one which parallels the freeway and the other which parallels the freeway as it bends and goes north to Sepulveda Pass. One is basically north-south, and the other about twenty-two and a half degrees turned toward the ocean. The public portion of the institution is on the public side, the freeway side, and the private portion is on the residential side, the sea side. The Getty Center sets up a dialogue between the street grid of Los Angeles and the hilltop. When you go to the museum, you will find the pavilions on the street-grid or freeway line and the buildings for temporary exhibitions on the Sepulveda Pass line. Shifting the axis also creates a dynamism between the buildings.

You finally came up with a Mediterranean model.

I don't know whether it is so much of a Mediterranean model. I think the model is more of a clusteral building, much like a college campus. Such as one sees at the University of Virginia by Thomas Jefferson, where the outdoor spaces are spaces you move through as you go from one building to another.

The travertine stone and the forms that support the hill make it look like a castle or a medieval hilltop village.

The stone has different connotations for different people. I see the stone as expressing the public portion, the museum and all the retaining walls, and the metal panels expressing the more private portions.

The complex looks like an homage to European civilization as it is incorporated in the Acropolis in Athens ...

No, it's not really an Acropolis. If it were an Acropolis it

The Getty Center and its various institutions tower over Los Angeles like a hilltop castle and village.

Arrival square and tram-stop. View
to the east of the auditorium, and the
North and West Buildings, which
house the institutes of information,
scholarships, education and
restoration.

The hill in the Brentwood villa district
before excavations began.

Model of the Getty Center.

The Getty Center as a major building
site.

*would be turned outward to the city, but it is turned inward to itself. And therefore it
is more of a monastic institution than an acropolis.*

You are well known as a defender of Modernism. Modernism was a northern
movement, whereas your Getty Center is inspired by a southern way of life, with
a lot of sun and spending much of the day outside. Did you experience any
tension between the two?

*The climate in Southern California is unique. And it is cer-
tainly more southern than the climate in New York. It is this climate that conditioned
the sense of moving inside and outside more than the idea that it is related to the
Mediterranean.*

How are these movements between inside and outside staged?

*If you are in a gal-
lery you can go out to the courtyard and come back into a gallery. Each gallery has
clusters of a small group of gallery spaces which are experienced. Then you move
out and you see a part of the landscape and a bit of the gardens. This relationship between interior and exterior space is very much a part of the uniqueness of this institution. The existing Getty Museum in Malibu already allowed you to walk from garden
to gallery to garden. We transferred that concept here.*

Do you consider your design to be a microcosm of Western civilization, as is some-times said?

No. The Getty is an extraordinary institution. And this institution has many aspects. And it is all of these aspects coming together in one place which is the nature of the Getty Center.

In many of your buildings you used the metaphor of the ship. Here it is the meta-phor of the castle or, as you say, of the monastery. Has Western culture to be defended?

I don't know whether it has to be defended. I think it is open. The Getty Center is a way of seeing Western civilization and understanding it and knowing about it. But I think that the freeway side, which is the side people see from their car as you move by at forty miles an hour, has one aspect, and when you are within the Center there is a human scale and openness which is very different.

What would be the American aspect in your design?

It is the openness, the flexibil-ity, the transparency that exist in America, the quality of large and small-scale spaces, the intimacy of some spaces and the public aspect of other spaces. So it perhaps has something for everyone. People ask me what will people remember when they come here? I think different people will remember different things. It depends on them. Some will remember the French painting galleries, some the fountains, others the views and the experience of being here.

View to the north, terrace in front of the café.

View to the west, footpath from the East Building to the auditorium.

56

Thinking of similar museums: the Louisiana Museum in Denmark tries to connect inside and outside as well. Where would you make a distinction to the Getty Center?

The scale is very different. The Louisiana museum in its original size was one piece of the Getty. The Getty is far larger. The location is totally different. The relationship of gallery to garden is a different kind of relationship. It doesn't look like the Louisiana museum. But having the outside part of the interior experience is similar.

Entrance to the research institute.

The Getty Center is a rather solitary a place on a Brentwood hilltop. How did you relate to nature and to the city?

As you move through the spaces you see the city in a way you don't see it from any other public place in all over Los Angeles. And you are more a part of Los Angeles here than you would be in any downtown street corner where you are just part of that block. So I think the uniqueness of this site is its accessibility, its visibility and its relationship to the city.

And how do you relate to the surrounding landscape?

We relate to nature by the way in which the building is on the hill, by the way in which you move out from the building onto the hill, the way in which the gardens and the interior spaces are interrelated. Basically we have cut into the hill, put in the building and then pushed the hill back around where it was. And so it is really growing out of the hillside in the form that the hill was before we began.

The Getty is more a village, not just a museum. How are the different parts connected?

First of all the entire building is interconnected underground. What we see is only half of the building. Half is below ground. The interaction that exists below ground is totally hidden. There are service quarters and mechanical connections.

And above ground?

Above ground it is the spaces between the buildings which are so important and they are thought out as carefully as the spaces within the building. For example the building that faces the freeway takes the form of a big arc, which fits the contour of the hill. The same arc is there at the arrival plaza when you get off the tram. The research institute's building forms a corresponding arc. And the big rotunda of the entrance hall of the museum is a comment on the research centre.

The circular entrance hall to the museum pavilions.

The inner courtyard between the museum pavilions, reflected in one of the many glass façades.

Exhibition galleries in the J. Paul Getty Museum (from left to right): the classical picture galleries are painted in colours or covered in fabric, the sculpture hall extends over two storeys, and the galleries for decorative art, here of the 18th century, were treated in period.

The museum has several pavilions itself. Does it reflect the Getty village as a whole?

I don't think the museum is a metaphor for the whole. The museum is its own thing. And from the very beginning it was John Walsh, the director, who wanted to break down the scale of the museum into a series of pavilions. This was part of the programme when we began. It wasn't a singular building but one which had connections and would allow different experiences. We clustered five different gallery pavilions around a series of courtyards and connected them by walkways.

Is the Getty museum a model for a museum of today?

The complex expresses the nature of the Getty and the Getty is a unique institution. Now whether every institution should look this way, I don't think so. Each museum is different. Its collection is different, its relation to the city and the experience it gives. And I don't think the Getty is a metaphor for what all museums should be like.

What is the architect's task when building a museum?

Most important is to make the works of art visible and look good. I think we succeeded in that here.

The Getty is a very specific museum. Its collection stops at 1900. Being a modernist architect, how did you adjust your style?

I don't think because the collection deals with sixteenth-, seventeenth- and eighteenth-century art, it has to be a sixteenth-, seventeenth- or eighteenth-century building.

But the Getty tried to transform it. Star designer Thierry W. Despont was engaged. He put fabric onto the gallery walls. Your colour is white, all the galleries are painted.

Yes, but that'll change.

So you can live with it?

Yes, I think it looks good. Some galleries are better than others but I think that the coloured walls look good with the paintings.

The Getty Center made a lot of other restrictions. Could you nevertheless realize your central ideas?

It wasn't easy all the time. But we managed to get together and understand what we were doing here in a way that everyone focused on what is the nature of this place and how can we best express it. Both in terms of the programmes as well as in the architecture.

You stand for white metal panels. Here you use roughly broken stone. Was the stone required by the Getty?

No, I wanted to use stone from the beginning. And I thought that stone expressed the nature of this institution: its permanence, its solidity and its durability.

Did you have the collection in mind when you were designing?

Yes, we knew the collection and the rooms are cut for the collection.

You gave them a special lighting system.

We developed the toplit system in order to bring daylight into all the gallery spaces and make it so that natural daylight didn't go on the wall where the paintings were hanging. The louvre system is very simple. It is in one position in the morning which keeps the direct light out and in the afternoon it flips and keeps the direct light out and at any time you can look up and see blue sky. So the idea was throughout the daylight hours you can move through the galleries and see the paintings totally illuminated with natural light.

The gallery rooms are surprisingly high.

Not for the scale of the paintings. I like the height and I like the way the light comes in.

How do you guide visitors?

You are guided by the relationship of the pavilions one to another. But what is most important is that there is no one route. You can make a choice. You can go one place or you can go another place. Always you have diversity. You can walk through the pavilions clockwise and see the collections in chronological order. Or you can go directly into the photography gallery or to the gallery for seventeenth century Dutch art. And if you want to see decorative arts you can go there. There is no hierarchy.

There are a lot of little things that distract me from looking at the exhibits. I can look outside, where there is water, rough stone walls, skylight and grand views. Is art acceptable only in little doses?

No. I like the distractions because I think you look at the works of art, you look inside and then you go outside. So you don't get museum fatigue. It is not a hermetically sealed experience as many museums are in a sort of exhaustedness, no place to go. Here you go out, sit by the water and then you go back in again.

Can you compare the Getty to the High Museum in Atlanta, the Museum of Decorative Arts in Frankfurt or the Museum of Contemporary Art in Barcelona, which you designed very recently?

They are each different: the collection, the location, the context. Besides that these three museums are all of a piece. There is a continuity within them. With the Getty Center the organization is based on discontinuity. For instance each of the museum's pavilions is different. The gallery spaces vary in scale. The relationship between gallery and circulation spaces is different, and the courtyards of the pavilions are different.

This being new for you, do you consider the Getty your major museum?

I think it is my major museum at the moment, yes.

Someone said, the new Getty Center was a place of collective solitude. Do you like this?

I think this is very good.

Robert Irwin's central garden complex with view of the museum pavilions.

Museum and Five Buildings for a Restaurant and Six Institutes

The existing J. Paul Getty Museum in Malibu had got too small for the works of art and the crafts collection, and the Getty Trust's other institutions were scattered all over Los Angeles. The new Getty Center brings all the various departments together on a hill in the high-class suburb of Brentwood on a site that offers the finest view of city, sea and mountains. From a distance the complex high above one of the large roads out of the city looks like a fortress, in which Western civilization is marking itself off from the multicultural metropolis. Anyone who goes up the hill on the electric railway comes to a generous piazza around which the museum and the institutes for research, restoration, education, information, museum management and scholarships are grouped. Richard Meier took away the top of the hill, put the whole complex in place and thrust the slopes back again, so that the Center seems to be growing out of the ground. The large volumes above ground are broken up by a number of openings and linked together formally. The yellowish-beige Travertine of the outer sections exudes honey-coloured warmth. The museum, which occupies the largest space, is itself split up into five pavilions, arranged around a courtyard complex. Foyers, staircases and walkways take up almost as much space in them as the exhibition galleries, whose pointed pyramid roofs give an open view of the blue Californian sky. No fixed route is prescribed, each pavilion is accessible from the outside, large areas of glass constantly open the interior up to the surrounding area. The walls of the exhibition galleries are covered with fabric or at least colourfully painted, to create a historically apt container for the collection of 16th- to 19th-century European painting, which swings between top-class and minor works, for the ancient sculptures, illuminated books and the French interiors. Richard Meier also forwent his preferred white walls for the world-class collection of photographs.

Location
1200 Getty Center Drive, Suite 400,
Los Angeles, CA 90049–1681, USA,
telephone +1 310 440 73 60

Client
The J. Paul Getty Trust, Los Angeles

Competition
1984

Construction
1987 (building work on museum began
1992-1997

Architects
Richard Meier & Partners, New York

Design
Richard Meier, Michael Palladino

Responsible partners
Richard Meier, Michael Palladino, Donald E.
Barker

Members of the team
John H. Baker, James Crawford, John Eisler,
Tom Graul, Michael Gruber,
Richard Kent Irving, Christine Kilian,
James Matson, James Mawson,
Milena Murdoch, A. Vic Schnider,
Timothy Shea, Richard Stoner, Aram Tatikian,
Laszlo Vito, J. F. Warren

General planning
Dinwiddie Construction Company

Project management consultants
Karsten/Hutman Margolf

Civil engineering
B & E Engineers, RBA Partners, Inc.

Geotechnical work
Woodward-Clyde Consultants

Earthworks
Pacific Englekirk, Inc.

Mechanical and electrical planning
Altieri Sebor Wieber, Hayakawa Associates

Lighting
Fisher Marantz Renfro Stone, Inc.

Museum exhibition galleries
Thierry W. Despont

Landscaping
Olin Partnership/Fong Associates, Emmet
L.Wemple & Associates, Dan Kiley Office

Central garden
Robert Irwin

Gross floor area, museum
11,000 m²

Exhibition area, museum
6,000 m²

Gross floor area, whole complex
87,800 m²

Gross floor area, institutes
46,900 m²

Gross floor area, services
40,900 m²

Building costs
1 billion US-$

Bibliography
Richard Meier, Building the Getty,
New York 1997.
John Walsh/Deborah Gribbon, The J. Paul
Getty Museum and Its Collections. A Museum
for the New Century, Los Angeles 1997.
The J. Paul Getty Trust, Making Architecture:
The Getty Center, London 1997.

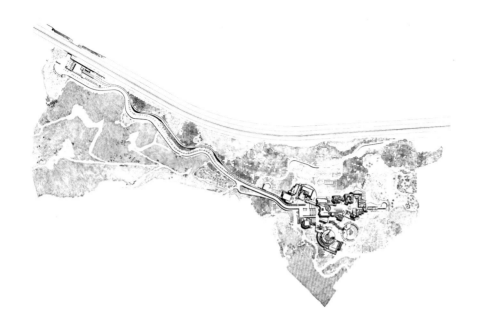

Site plan.

Ground floor plan.

The Almost Vanishing Museum

**Interview with Rafael Moneo on the Moderna and Arkitektur Museet
in Stockholm**

Mr Moneo, your building for the Moderna and Arkitektur Museet in Stockholm is a great success with the public. This is surprising in that it is almost invisible. Why did you hide it?

Rafael Moneo

I always thought building on Skeppsholmen meant maintaining the integrity of the island. Therefore our project was very much based on a clear strategy about the location. The choice of the site was crucial. I tried to merge the largest building on the island, which was the Tighuset, with the gymnasium, where the old Moderna Museet was, and by doing so I was taking a picture of this large elongated building by putting something beside it. That was the reason why I decided not to build near the shore but on the top of the island. The second important decision was about the fragmented construction of the building. This would maintain the fragmented pattern of the island as well as of Stockholm as a whole. This is the reason why each room identifies itself with the skylight. In a way it is almost like assembling and putting together a collection of different independent rooms. Thus we maintained something of the factory-like atmosphere that the island had. As you know Skeppsholmen was devoted to the navy. There were shipyards, warehouses and workshops. This varied character is reflected by the repetition of the skylights. So by using formal structures that play and live together with the trees and the other buildings on the island we produced a building that, as you said, is almost hidden.

Did this concept come to your mind already at your first visit to the island? You speak of "the murmur of the site" at the beginning of a project.

To tell you the truth, I didn't visit the island before doing the competition. I had been in Stockholm only once and I stayed there for one complete week. But that was in 1962. In those days I went on a trip to Scandinavia. I started in Göteborg and went to Stockholm, where I slept in the youth hostel boat. I was mainly seeing the work of Gunnar Asplund and went on to Finland where I visited Aalto. I was then working with Jørn Utzon in Denmark who had been Aalto's pupil. He sent me with a book for Aalto and I was able to spend a day in his office, talking with him. I even had an interview with him at that time. So for the competition of the Moderna Museet I worked with my memories of Skeppsholmen and hoped to recognize the things where they were. I always thought of the project in those terms. If you look at the model made for the competition you see that it was kept almost completely the same throughout the whole project.

Although it is 250 m long, Rafael Moneo has hidden the Museum of Modern Art and of Architecture behind the existing buildings on the Stockholm island of Skeppsholmen so skilfully that it is never possible to take in its full size.

The exhibition galleries can be identified from the outside by lanterns that give the museum a clear presence at night.

Rafael Moneo's long building skilfully picks up the architecture of the former Swedish naval base.

What were the changes like?

By putting the building on the top of the hill you establish a horizontal level for the visitors to the museum and yet you have the opportunity of creating two lower floors where the staff and all the facilities can easily be accomodated. In the very first stage of the competition we didn't design the architectural museum as an independent building. It was completely within the gymnasium which housed the Moderna Museet until then. But working on the project we realized that it needed something else and we added the wing of the architectural museum which is almost a quotation of contemporary architecture, a kind of homage to Swedish architecture of the thirties and forties. I also thought it would make a nice contrast and I liked the fact that it eliminated any monumentalist temptation.

There is a tension between the two museum buildings. For the Moderna Museet you excavated fifty thousand tons of stone, whereas the architecture museum is built around the rock.

This is true. What is important about the architecture museum are the open spaces, the courtyard. I also like the way in which the two new wings emphasize the classical façade of the former gymnasium between them.

You said the architecture museum was a homage to Scandinavian Modernism. The atmosphere in the Moderna Museet reminded me of Gunnar Asplund.

Could be, but not directly. I didn't see any direct relations. Obviously there are influences and all the memories you have about architecture. In the days of the competition I was working on the project of the museum for the Thyssen-Bornemisza collection in the Palacio de Villahermosa in Madrid. The pyramidal roofs with the skylights are very much connected to the skylights at the Thyssen Museum.

It's also Seville Airport, I think.

It could also be Seville, and obviously there are some references to Louis Kahn, for instance. But I didn't follow him strictly. In his Kimbell Art Museum geometry and regularity prevail. In Stockholm I wanted just the contrary. Though I was working with the same form I wanted variety and diversity. The other influences here in Stockholm are some very compact plans by Le Corbusier. I was thinking of the schemes of how to split the square without falling into the easy way to do it in nine square grids, but doing something more complex. Probably there are many other influences. Perhaps remotely even Asplund. My main experience was looking for this variety. By maintaining the same shape and changing the sizes I tried to find out whether variety was possible without being affected. The entire museum is breathing by changing the sizes. I like the experience that you are not disturbed by moving from one room to another. They have a nice fluidity.

The large hall near the vestibule can be used in various ways and is intended above all for touring exhibitions. The ceiling picks up the square basic grid of the galleries.

Exhibition gallery with typical ceiling rising as a pyramid to the roof lantern.

The exhibition galleries stress their square module right down to the way in which the wooden floor is laid, but they are different in size and breathe through a spiral rhythm of large and small units.

What made me think of Asplund and his Stockholm library was the quiet, even classical atmosphere of the rooms of the Moderna Museet and that at the same time they form a maze, a labyrinth, when you walk around. In Asplund's library as well you have these meanderings and in the storage areas it is really a maze, but with a very strong rational order. Perhaps this is the overall impression your Stockholm museum gave me: it provides a very harmonic atmosphere, but at the same time there are a lot of little things that make it sharp.

I agree with that.

By establishing the intellectual agenda of a building in a way you are very much establishing bridges with the architecture you like. Mentioning Asplund you mentioned someone I admire very much.

Comparing your building with other entries in the competition, Tadao Ando proposed a big scenic arrangement down the hill to the shore.

The entrance hall with its light-well gives access to the Art and Architecture Museum like a piazza.

Ando was more monumental. Probably he was thinking of something that maintains the idea of the museum as a temple. Even though you can identify this touch of classicism or historical architecture in our own project there is no monumentalization at all nor any sanctification of the museum as an institution. That seems to me to be one of the most positive issues in our design. Here you will not expect to find a museum that by itself almost works like a cathedral. Just the contrary. The museum as an institution is dissolved in the building and the building in turn is taken over by the city as a whole. I like to give visitors the sensation that being in the museum is almost like being in the city as a whole. The institution is absorbed by the city. It holds it. This is a nice way of making works of art accessible. I am pleased with this. So even if the building might not look very much like a modern building it has a progressive approach to the subject of museums by giving up the temptation of sanctifying the institution. A museum

that does not intimidate seems to me appropriate for the Scandinavian culture. It means approaching art in a frame that does not create any sense of overwhelming power.

The exhibitions galleries with their peaceful atmosphere are conceived above all for the art of classical Modernism.

You spoke of dissolving the building in the urban context. On the other hand the Moderna Museet has a strong presence of its own. It is almost like two concepts of space being brought together.

Probably you are right. It is very difficult for example to take photographs of the building that are not related to the island as a whole. But each room is longing for the integrity and sense of unity to be found in classical architecture. In a way I am trying to be extremely synthetic by designing space that is the source of the light and at the same time establishes the roof and the walls. In a way it is almost like saying I have a piece of architecture that is so appropriate to its function that a strict continuity emerges between the source of light and the walls. I like to compare these rooms with lamps: it is almost like being inside a lamp. You don't recognize very clearly where the source of light is. Light comes together with and is the result of the architectural phenomenon. The skylight almost is the room, you do not separate the room and the roof from the light.

In some way it is the long corridor, not the galleries, which forms the backbone of the whole complex, the air, the light, the void.

No doubt about it. In the restaurant and some of the galleries you have views of the city. With the corridor you have a centre and you are very much absorbed by the character of the island. It establishes the connection with the elongated Tighuset. The space between the two buildings is very important. But the corridor also provides you with different choices which I appreciate very much. It allows you to go either to the hall for temporary exhibitions or to one of the three clusters for the collection, whatever you prefer.

An over 100 m long corridor with ribbon windows forms the spine of the whole complex, giving access to the three clusters of museum galleries.

Your Stockholm museum touches a general problem as well: How can I build something that is sympathetic with the surroundings and nevertheless makes a figure, a "gestalt"?

I think we already talked about this in other terms. Yes, we have been using this powerful synthetic concept of gestalt, which is able to convey the solution for the urban conditions and at the same time for the works of art.

Art itself has many more possibilities to bring these contrasts together. A simple example of this would be the collage. Do you use art concepts when you design?

In this case I very much had in mind the collection of the Moderna Museet which is mainly traditional avant-garde, without many huge works. It is wonderful. And I always thought that our rooms could be clustered in a way that those clusters held the main divisions of the collection: the Swedish artists, who are much more interesting than one expects, and the traditional avant-garde artists. From the fifties onwards, Pontus Hulten bought a lot of outstanding pieces of the classical modern period and later on of the New York school. Nowadays the Moderna Museet has one of the best collections in Europe. Therefore I wanted all those pieces to be together. Later the museum has bought more contemporary art. Therefore we thought the collection could be grouped in the series of clusters we have. In addition there is a large space of 1,100 square metres for temporary exhibitions, which can be divided in many ways. As these exhibitions are considered crucial for the life of a museum we located this space close to the entrance. The diversity of the collection also explains why I wanted to keep the integrity and particularity of each school. You may enter a room showing one single piece or only the painters of a particular school and so retain the intensive single flavour of the room.

The new Architecture Museum building, adjacent to the central historical drill hall, surprisingly falls back on the language of Nordic Modernism.

You use serial elements for the building. What is your interest in them?

That is a bit of a problem: I myself always resist repetition. I don't like architecture that is based on an overrating of logic and intrusive economy that would be connected to modular structure and repetition. In the Stockholm museum, even though repetition is a given, I insist so much on those changes in proportion and sizes that they prevent us from seeing the building as repetition. I wouldn't like the building being seen as an exercise in working with two or three sizes. We have used many more units anyway.

What do you think of the idea of a museum being a workshop, like the old Moderna Museet proposed?

I can only talk in very personal terms here. I still enjoy going to museums whose permanent collection I know well. I go there and enjoy the pieces I like.

Ground plan of the entrance level (3rd floor).

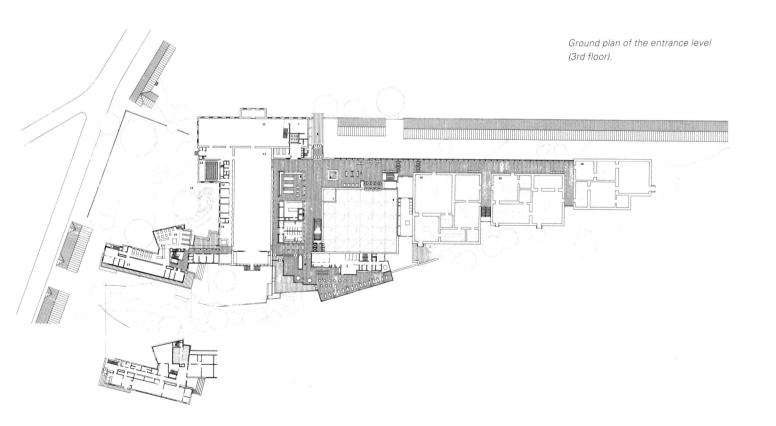

New Building and Conversion for Two Museums

A museum could scarcely be more reticent on the outside. The new double museum for modern art and for architecture on the Stockholm island of Skeppsholmen has 19,500 m² of usable floor space and is 250 m long. Rafael Moneo built it at the highest point of the island, and yet almost hid it between the low buildings of the former naval base. The island is not to be dominated, but reinforced in its particular qualities. The red-painted Moderna Museet changes its face as the viewers change their position. Seen from the nearby shore it closes itself off like a towering eyrie, with a glazed restaurant thrusting up like a viewing cockpit. It presents its elegantly plain portico to the drive on the island side. In between, three volumes, in which the galleries are arranged in clusters, mark the run of the edge of the slopes and snuggle up to the long Tighuset on the land side, with a glazed corridor rather like a single-storey pavilion. The white-rendered new building for the Arkitektur Museet, which was added only in the course of the planning process, forms a contrast by playfully varying the relaxed language of Scandinavian Modernism. Moneo's double museum is neither a temple nor a demonstration of power. The axis of the building is the corridor, which is over 100 m long, and thus an empty space. It provides access to three clusters of galleries and the 1,100 m² space for temporary exhibitions. The 19 exhibition rooms have light wooden floors, and are based on a strictly square grid, but they vary in size and character and are tailored precisely to the high-calibre collection of classical Modern and Scandinavian art. Lanterns, to which the ceilings rise like pyramids, provide daylight, but the curators have restricted it considerably. The few windows frame surrounding nature and make it into pictures. The magnificent view is reserved largely for the museum restaurant, which is entered through the great entrance piazza and links the two museums. A temporary exhibition gallery is available for contemporary art, and there are a cinema and windowless rooms for video works on the first basement level.

Location
Skeppsholmen, 10327 Stockholm, Sweden, telephone +46 8 519 552 00

Client
National Property Board of Sweden (Statens Fastighetsverk)

Competition
1991

Construction
1995–1997

Architects
José Rafael Moneo Vallés, Madrid

Projekt architects
Belén Moneo, Jeff Brock

On-site architect
Max Holst

Members of the team
Fernando Iznaola, Ignacio Quemada, Eduardo Belzunce, Michael Bischoff, Robert Robinowitz, Lucho Marcial

Associate architects
White Architects AB

Members of the team
Björn Norén, Viljar Päss, Anna Karin Edlbom, Magnus Croon, Mats Anslöv, Lars-Erik Karlsson, Louise Masreliez

Structural engineering
Byggkonsult AB

Mechanical engineering
Energo AB

Electrical engineering
Wo-Konsult AB

Lighting design
KTH Arkitektur/belysningslära

Lighting
Fisher Marantz Renfro Stone

Security
Team TSP Konsult AB

Fire safety
Brandskyddslaget BOTAB AB

Acoustics
Ingemanssons Akustik

Theatre experts
Arteno Arkitektur & Teater

Interior design: public areas
Rafael Moneo, Belén Moneo, Jeff Brock

Interior design: restaurants, bookshops, shop
Thomas Sandell

Interior design: offices
Karen Nyrén

General contractor
NCC AB

Total gross floor area
25,600 m²

Gross floor area, Moderna Museet
19,300 m²

Gross floor area, Arkitektur Museet
6,300 m²

Exhibition area, Moderna Museet
4,500 m²

Exhibition area, Arkitektur Museet
1,500 m²

Building costs
450 million skr

Bibliography
Rafael Moneo, El Croquis 64, 1994.
Peter Nigst, Rafael Moneo: Bauen für die Stadt, Stuttgart 1993.
Arkitekturmuseet, Moneo, Stockholm 1993.
arkitektur 2/1998, Stockholm.

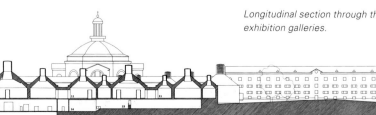

Longitudinal section through the exhibition galleries.

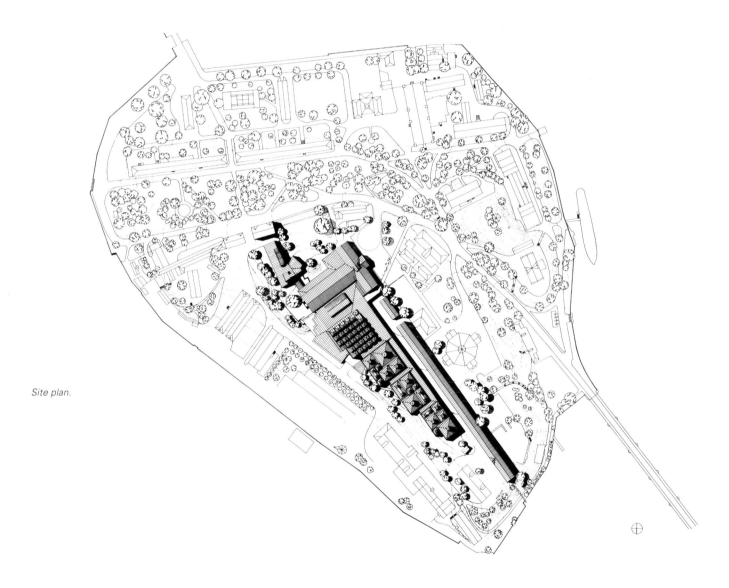

Site plan.

Sea side elevation.

The Museum as an Exhibition Machine

Interview with Jean Nouvel on the Culture and Congress Centre in Lucerne

M. Nouvel, what are your views about the Centre Georges Pompidou?

I think that the Beaubourg is very important as a historical building. It symbolizes the architecture of the seventies. It is a piece of realized Archigram, even though it doesn't live like an Archigram building now. It is a kind of supporting architecture that shows its infrastructure. It represents a strategy of taking up and combining many things. It needs a lot of signs and a lot of events to complement it. Today this structure is lived a bit too academically.

Jean Nouvel

You have built a lot of cultural centres. Do they relate to the Beaubourg?

No, I don't think there is anything in common there. Think of a building like the Fondation Cartier. It's a cultural location, as it puts on contemporary exhibitions, but not a museum, not a building to house a collection. It is in fact a space with great potential, an empty space in which everyone can do as they wish. It they want to put up walls they put up walls, if they don't, they don't. If they want to open up the space and be outside they can do that as well. That means that whenever you go there you're going to a different place. People sometimes think that the building was intended to stay the same. But that is not the case. It is a very radical concept. There is almost no supporting architecture. It's different at the Beaubourg. The Fondation Cartier is designed in such a way that it can't be left as it is, while with the Beaubourg people like leaving it is it is. The Beaubourg also reveals its structural system. The Cartier is the opposite. It makes the structure disappear.

Where would you place the new Cultural and Congress Centre in Lucerne in this field of tension?

There is a very precise brief for the museum in Lucerne. Unlike other places where this or that piece has to make its impact, our design is not aimed at a specific collection. The galleries are very reduced, well proportioned and rectangular. Good natural lighting is fundamental. The architecture has to be as neutral as possible – in other words quite classical by today's standards. But that follows a Swiss museum tendency.

Did you design the exhibition galleries for the museum yourself? Was it your idea to use a grid for them?

Yes. I always wanted to have this large, flexible area. We worked with the previous curator, who brought in Rémy Zaugg as an advisor, with my agreement. We decided together on the most extreme and demanding variant, for a geometry that is as regular as possible: the rooms consist of one or two modules. The doors are relatively small openings in the large white walls. The toplit ceilings diffuse the sunlight from the southern aspect, and are made of transparent

The Lucerne Culture and Congress Centre is bordered on two sides by Lake Lucerne. Jean Nouvel stages a dialogue between the building, the water and the surrounding mountains and opens it up to the neighbouring old town and the lake promenade opposite. Three buildings for the concert hall, congress centre and art museum are held together by the dominant roof, which emphasizes the horizontal.

material. Rémy Zaugg wanted to keep the architecture as fine and simple as possible. I don't know whether to use the word "minimal", as it was coined in relation to art. But in Lucerne the ideal of a supporting role for architecture is absolutely central.

That is very different from the Institut du Monde Arabe (IMA), where the rooms are sometimes very low, sometimes very high, and establish a strong rhythm.

The Lucerne museum is very different, although I wasn't able to plan for a specific collection at IMA either. That was a great disappointment. In the case of IMA we didn't know the collections because the Louvre lent the objects in the first place, but they soon went back again and the Arab countries are now showing other exhibits. And so I designed an ensemble that is put together like an informative table in a book. All the objects can be changed. And you can show them in whatever chronology you like. Of course visitors should not notice this. The galleries are intended to seem as though they were designed for the very objects that you see in them. These can be sculptures, plates, little faience pieces, calligraphy, carpets etc.

What does an architect have to do when building a museum?

The first duty of a museum is to show what there is to be shown. This applies to the Fondation Cartier as well. When I think that critics reproached me for only thinking of my building it

makes my hair stand on end. Where are the walls?, people ask. But that is precisely the point. Artists have to build the walls! – A lot of artists want walls and a lot don't. No architecture is there for its own sake as far as I am concerned. Architecture always responds to a precise problem. It is the curator, not the architect who has the programme and the legitimacy in matters affecting art. I have never imposed an architectural ideology on a museum. Should one build a space that actually isn't a space, in which everything is possible, or should one create a place that artists have to come to terms with? That is the eternal question in museum building. I don't think there is an answer to it. The more multi-functional a place is and the better it wants to accommodate contradictory things, the more you are moving towards a non-space that has to be re-created every time. The architect has to create conditions to make that easier.

Your museums are usually part of a cultural centre. Do you intend to show art as part of a general expression of culture?

Unfortunately I did not make this choice.

The façade design refers to the structure of the building: the section for the concert hall is red and the corridors suspended in front of it are painted blue and play with the ship metaphor.

The briefs for the projects always laid down that the museum was part of a cultural centre. I think that's a good thing incidentally, in the case of IMA, for example. But that doesn't mean that a museum can't exist in its own right. But if that's the case, then the question arises of what are all these museums trying to say? Culture has today taken the place of cult. Art has become a kind of substitute religion; priest's sermon or the artist's message – something of that kind. Of course that isn't a particularly original thought. Today the real problem for me is one of creating places for art in life and in the city once more. Art is not really in the city in a museum. That is art in a safe. That is art in a cemetery. That is not art in a condition of freedom.

Are you against museums?

We need museums. Don't say that I am against museums! But we need things other than museums. Art's place should not only be in the museum. Art must be a greater presence in our daily lives and public spaces. There are no more direct connections with architecture because artists have started to feel the cold more and are increasingly isolating themselves. They want people to see their work without having anything else around it. I hope that these principles will start to be questioned at the beginning of the new century. And I am looking for conceptual formulations that will make architecture and art able to work together again, a renaissance.

How can that be implemented in the Cultural and Congress Centre in Lucerne?

I am working in a very traditional framework in Lucerne. It could not be more traditional. It is an institutional museum that will show parts of the collection and touring temporary exhibitions. Here I am playing the part of an architect who is building a classical museum. What they want from me is a machine for contemporary art exhibitions, using the resources that are available today. That means: good proportions, white walls, good light, variable spaces for the paintings. Here architecture is a reticent device for showing art. Now my problem is to give this museum a presence of its own. We have used various things to this end: the city can be seen in the background; it is very quiet; a game is played with a certain rhythm. But it is a game with almost nothing. It is the opposite of Bilbao, where Frank Gehry has successfully created a space for the exhibits intended for show there. There is a real dialogue between the architect and the art there. In Lucerne I am not in that kind of situation at all. Rather the contrary.

You have often said that your architecture is intended to give a place identity. How does that work in Lucerne?

Lucerne is a very unusual city with a very strong identity. The new building is intended to reinforce that identity even further. It plays with the lake, the water and the reflection of the light on the water. Its horizontals relate to the mountains. It is determined completely by the place, and complements the existing landmarks in the city. It includes a concert-hall that is so refined technically that you wouldn't find anything like it even in Paris. The multi-functional rooms open up the building for the people of Lucerne. The three components, the concert-hall, the congress hall and the museum are like three separate pieces of architecture under one roof.

You stress that the city presents itself as chaotic today. What function can a cultural centre have in it?

When I said that today's cities work on a chaos system, it's a statement that applies much more to cities other than Lucerne. Lucerne has been much protected. Industrial cities, particularly in the southern hemisphere, are growing at a phenomenal rate without any urban regulation. This urban growth logic fits in with chaos theory. The concept is not negative, but comes from mathematics. I am simply pointing out that one needs to know the system within which one is building. It is the opposite of the drawn and planned city, with many contradictions.

Where is the chaotic aspect in Lucerne?

Even though Lucerne is not a prototype of this kind of city, I feel here as well that an existing situation always has to be improved. A new building has to shape the existing chaos more positively – and to evaluate what will remain. This applies to cities that have developed very chaotically, but

The model makes clear how much the tripartite layout breaks up the large volume. A pool leads to the central entrance in the central section, which is set back, and takes two channels of water into the centre between the fingers of the building.

The Centre is cut off from Calatrava's adjacent station by aluminium grids of various thicknesses suspended in front of a glass façade. This section houses the art museum's exhibition galleries as well as the catering facilities on the top floor.

Central entrance with pool, forecourt, open terrace and flanking staircase towers. The central section of the building is bluish-grey, and the concert hall section bottle green. The windows in the almost floating concrete building are cut very much on the diagonal and capture the surroundings in images from the inside.

View of the white concert hall with 1840 seats. Its outstanding acoustics were created in co-operation with Russell Johnson.

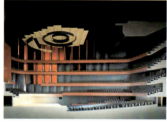

First colour concept for the concert hall.

to Lucerne as well. The Cultural and Congress Centre is in a particular situation: there is Calatrava's station, the large and very ordinary post office building behind it, and neither of them relate to the city. So the Cultural Centre has to mediate between the old town, which you can see from my building, and the part of the city that the old town sees from its bank. It relativizes the force of the station and the post office. I am not looking for integration in the classical sense of the word, but for a different logic and different power for buildings that are growing old together.

How is it that cultural buildings have this particular ability to integrate?

A museum or a cultural centre has a unique urban presence. They are intended to be inviting. When you look at all these cultural buildings, whether it is the cultural centre in Tours, the Opéra in Lyon, the Fondation Cartier, IMA, they are all intended to fulfil this purpose. And Lucerne as well. The water that goes into the building, this roofed square and much more all offer an invitation.

How important is art for your work as an architect? Are you trying to bring the two together?

Art has always played a large part in my life. I originally wanted to be a painter, but then decided against it. I think that art's relationship with architecture has changed completely and that a different form of language has to be found for the two to communicate. This can be only on a conceptual plane. There are no longer simple rules of the kind that there used to be in the 19th century or previously, when art had a precisely defined place in terms of architecture. And it is no longer possible to be content with an attitude that was important in the twentieth century, according to which things happen autonomously and do not relate to each other; a kind of collage. It's important now to find conceptual strategies so that we can start working together again.

Computer simulation of a museum gallery with light ceiling and doorways.

Would it help in this situation to create places that are not museums, but completely open spaces for artists?

I believe that the problem is not about creating an open place for artists. What we have to do is find a place or a strategy for bringing art back into the places where we live, and to be aware that it is not only intended for the market. We have to find a much more natural relationship again.

Has any of your buildings done that successfully?

No, I can't say that, although I have worked with artists on some buildings. I try to create conditions that are favourable to such encounters.

The grid façade of the museum wing lends detail to the large wall area with the varying distances between the bars and creates a sophisticated interplay of transparency and opacity.

Where do you think museums will be in the next century?

I can't give a clear answer to that, I want museums to become less necessary. For that would mean that art has reconquered its natural place in society. Perhaps the museum of the 21st century should invest more money in living art, so that it can be breathed into people's lives. But there will always be museums, and indeed there always must be. But there must be something else as well: an access to works of art that is much more natural and direct.

View of the new concert hall. The roof protrudes by 25 m on the open lake side, and by as much as 35 m towards Europaplatz.

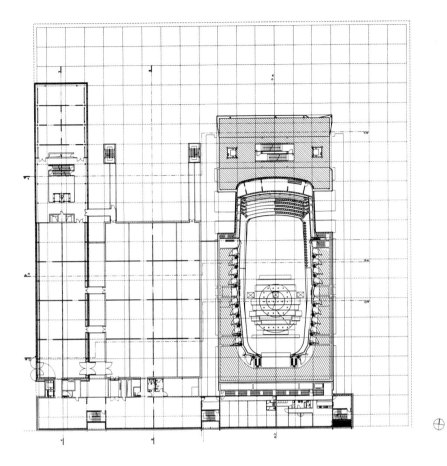

Ground plan, exhibition gallery level in the art museum.

East-West section.

Section through the concert hall.

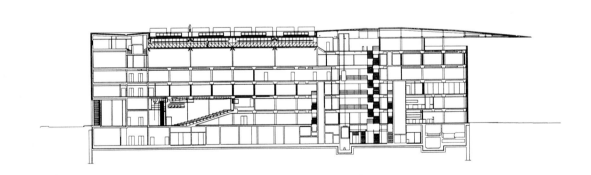

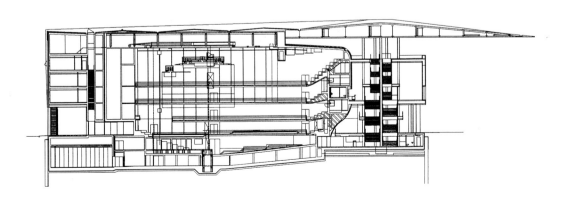

Concert Hall, Congress Rooms and Art Gallery

The new Cultural and Congress Centre in Lucerne brings together a concert hall (conceived for the International Music Festival Weeks), a congress centre and the municipal art gallery. Jean Nouvel makes these very different requirements into the architectural theme of his design in an interplay of enclosure and transparency. The starting-point is the extraordinary site on the shore of Lake Lucerne. The building presents itself almost monolithically to the adjacent station and post office, which are both large buildings. But it opens up in a variety of ways to the lake, the quayside facilities, the 19th-century hotel blocks and the small scale of the historical old town on the other side of the lake. The three parallel volumes of the concert and congress halls, and the multi-functional rooms between them appear independent and are different in form, colour and texture from the outside. The waters of the lake thrust deep into the complex via a pool and canals. The main entrance and the foyer shift backwards in the face of it. A 23 m high roof protrudes up to 35 m over the forecourt and holds the three sections of the building together, assisted by a rear transverse section housing the service areas. The edge of the roof includes a fine, draughtsmanly horizon line that responds to the silhouette of the surrounding mountains. Light reflected from the surface of the water plays on the underside of the roof. Jean Nouvel stages the common features and different elements of the institutions right down to the last detail, and likewise grandiose nature's mountains and lake. The concert-hall has very refined acoustics, and its timber cladding makes it reminiscent of a musical instrument, sitting within the envelope of the building like a self-contained concrete body. The central hall is designed for variation, and a terrace opens on to the square and the lake. The art gallery occupies the level above the congress centres and the central area. Placing it directly under the roof makes it possible to provide toplighting from glazed ceilings for the exhibition galleries, which number over 20. They are connected to each other without corridors by various routes, but can also be handled as little enfilades, so that it is possible to present chronologically retrospective exhibitions as well as exhibitions with a thematic focus. Structuring them in three sections – over the congress wing, the central area and the transverse link at the back – also makes it possible to show large parts of the collection and temporary exhibitions next to each other, to which the building owes its international reputation. The galleries themselves, on whose conception Rémy Zaugg also worked, are plain exhibition boxes with relatively small doorways and without any external link; a small number of views out and through enable visitors to find their way. Access to the museum floor is through a two-storey hall entered from the station side.

Location
Europaplatz, 6005 Luzern, Switzerland, telephone +4141 210 36 46

Client
Trägerstiftung Kultur- und Kongreßzentrum Luzern (City and Canton of Lucerne, private individuals)

Competition
1989

Project
1993

Construction
1995–2000 (concert-hall opening 1998)

Architect
Architectures Jean Nouvel, Paris

Project architect
Brigitte Metra

Members of the team
Joelle Achache, Marie Hélene Baldran, Didier Brault, Sandro Carbone, Gunther Domenig, Xavier Lagurgue, Denis Laurent, Philippe Mathieu, Eric Nespoulos, Julie Parmentier, Mathias Raasch, Markus Roethlisberger, Beth Weinstein, Stefan Zopp

General Contractor
Arge Totalunternehmer: Elektrowatt, Göhner Merkur AG, Zürich

Structural engineering
Elektrowatt Ingenieurunternehmung AG, Zürich, Plüss + Meyer Bauingenieure, Lucerne

Electrical engineering
Scherler AG, Lucerne

Climate control design
Balduin Weisser AG, Lucerne

Sanitary planning
M. Schudel Ing. SIA, Winterthur

Lighting engineering
Scherler AG, Lucerne

Acoustic consultants
ARTEC, Russell Johnson

Scenic consultant
Jacques Le Marquet

Museum consultant
Rémy Zaugg

Colour design
Alain Bony

Total gross floor area
35,000 m^2

Total usable floor area
22,000 m^2

Gross floor area, museum
3,600 m^2

Exhibition area, museum
2,500 m^2

Gross floor area, concert hall
2,350 m^2 (1,840 seats)

Gross floor area, congress centre
2,100 m^2

Gross floor area, middle hall
1,450 m^2

Total cost
200 million SFr.

Total building cost
160 million SFr.

Bibliography
Karl Bühlmann, Kultur- und Kongreßzentrum Luzern, Lucerne/Rotkreuz 1998.
Olivier Boissière, Jean Nouvel, Basel/Boston/Berlin 1996.
Olivier Boissière, Jean Nouvel, Paris 1996.

Model of the urban situation between the lake,
the old town and the adjacent large buildings.

The Museum as a Safe

Interview with Renzo Piano on the Museum for the Fondation Beyeler in Basel

Mr Piano, how did you get in touch with Ernst Beyeler, and then win the contract for the museum?

Renzo Piano

Ernst Beyeler rang the office. Then he came to Paris. That must be over ten years ago now. He talked to me about museums in general and my own museum projects – he mentioned the Centre Pompidou, of course, but he was most interested in the Menil Collection in Houston. He wanted to know a great deal about the working processes that generate our projects. We discussed a different location first. Finally we looked at the site on the Berower estate in Riehen and started our actual work on the project.

The press talked about close co-operation. How did that work?

When someone like Ernst Beyeler wants to build a museum he is most concerned to find someone he can work well with. It's a question of chemistry, of communication. A museum like that is also a portrait of the owner.

Were you asked to design certain things and to leave others?

No. Of course, as an architect you have to understand your client's mental world. But Ernst Beyeler is very cultivated. He doesn't say do this or do that. It was like a table-tennis match. We talked about drawings and models and after a while no one knew who was contributing what to the game. Individual thoughts mingle.

What were important common interests?

Ernst Beyeler was very interested in natural lighting. The light was not to be fixed or static. It must be able to change, so that the works of art come to life. Perception was to change during the day, in different weather and with the seasons. The building is in a park, after all. You feel changing nature very directly there.
As well as this we wanted to design a building that was absolutely up-to-date technically. For example, energy consumption was important to Ernst Beyeler – not just because energy-saving is in at the moment in Europe. Not using too much energy is part of his building ethic.

What aims did you pursue in your building?

Ernst Beyeler summed up our aims in a very lovely formulation: "I want luxe, calme et volupté". He borrowed the phrase from Matisse, by whom he has some very fine works.

View into the Giacometti Gallery at the Fondation Beyeler. Renzo Piano constantly relates the art to the surrounding landscaped park in his building.

West façade: Renzo Piano designed a low pavilion for the Fondation, with a complex light ceiling floating above it like a magic carpet.

The museum is fitted in between the two walls surrounding the Berower-park on the fringe of the Basel suburb of Riehen: four parallel walls, each seven metres apart, are clad with porphyry on the outside and create a three-aisled exhibition area.

What did he mean by it?

Luxe doesn't mean magnificence, but a very high standard for materials and the way they are used. Calme is easy to understand for a museum. A little anecdote might cast some light on volupté: I was standing with Ernst in the gallery with Monet's water-lily painting recently, and the sun started to cast some very slight reflections from the pool outside through the panes and on to the walls of the room. That is a piece of volupté.

You were looking for a particular atmosphere with your design.

Yes, immaterial qualities above all, like cheerfulness, contemplation, the vibration of light, the opening into the park. Fixing the number of square metres was certainly the easiest thing. It was more difficult to anchor the museum in the history of museum-building since the Second World War. Many museums are mere self-fulfilment, rather than serving art. They show only themselves. That was out of the question for Ernst Beyeler's collection from the outset. This museum is intended to be geared entirely to looking at art. That isn't as simple to achieve as it sounds. You can't just build neutral white spaces, as the "white cubes" argument suggests. They kill works of art just as much as hyperactive spaces that make the museum building into a piece of self-indulgence. We wanted to make the building as good as the most recent technology would allow for preserving and keeping works of art. That is ultimately what a museum is about. A museum is a Florentine palazzo for preserving art. And secondly it's a place for looking at art. For that reason we wanted to have natural light, and at the same time the best possible technology, which we used for optimal energy use and for the awnings that filter the sunlight. Here we could go back to experience that we had gained from the Menil Collection in Houston and other museums. And of course our London engineering partners Ove Arup & Partners were a big help here.

*A water-lily pool borders the museum on the south side
and reflects sunlight into the galleries.*

Monet's painting of water-lilies with the water-lily pool.

Oceanic sculptures complement the Fondation Beyeler's Classical Modern collection.

The new museum is a building for the art of classical Modernism, for Picasso, Matisse, Cézanne, Giacometti, but also Baselitz. Did this collection make particular demands on the architecture?

Definitely. If you think of the Menil Collection, for instance, there are ten thousand works there stored in the conservation safe on the roof of the building, then they are occasionally brought down and exhibited for a few months. The Beyeler Collection includes two hundred fantastic works that are all permanently on show. This makes quite different demands on protecting the works. They have no time to rest in a store.
We also developed the individual galleries from the works of art. Take the Giacometti gallery, for example. When we started work on the Beyeler Museum we built a room here in Paris on a scale of 1 : 10, reproduced every Giacometti sculpture in the collection on the same scale and put them in this room to test it. Or Monet's water-lilies: they were intended for the room by the pool from the beginning. You can look at the water there, and it vibrates lightly and reflects the sunlight. That only works if the pool of water is on the south side, otherwise the water remains dead.

There was a delay of one year before completion. Why was that?

There was no definite reason for it. It you're building a factory or an office block, you have to hurry. It's different with a museum. That is the materialization of a dream. The main thing is to make it turn out well.

And what effect did that have?

The building is perfectly executed. When you go into other museums, you see smoke detectors, signs, surveillance cameras and other things all over the place. You can't see any of that in the Riehen museum. It's all simple and flat. That took a lot of time. It took four months simply to persuade the fire brigade that the smoke detectors could be in rather than on the wall.

You've put a filigree roof on walls that are clad with red stone. Are you fond of contradictions like this?

It's not a contradiction, it's a contrast. And that is part of the project. The museum is intended to be part of the earth, like a romantic ruin. We achieve that with stone walls. They are part of the place and seem as though they have always been there. We have planted a lot of ivy, and that will enhance this effect. The roof is like a magic carpet, but it works as a filter. White, with a lot of glass, very light, a wonderful piece of engineering and a glass sculpture at the same time. We wanted to create this state of tension.

That sounds very romantic.

Perhaps it is. But I see it above all as a combination between regional and universal connections in good architecture. The museum is firmly anchored in its location. But the requirements for lighting and energy technology are valid everywhere where museums are built. We have to accept this kind of complexity. This building shows how that is possible.

How did you link the Beyeler museum with the Basel region?

It picks up the two longitudinal walls of the park in which it is sited. We placed four long walls between them. At first I wanted to use the typical Basel stone as well. But it is not very long-lasting and therefore it is less well suited for a building intended to last for ever. So we looked for a similar stone that is more durable.

Do you really believe that this museum will last for ever?

Of course not, but almost. It is very well built and can be maintained very easily. And museums are always built in a logic of eternity. The collector wants to pass his work on to the future like an artist. I remember President Georges Pompidou receiving Richard Rogers and me to talk about the cultural centre in Paris. Richard was wearing a red shirt, and I had a t-shirt under my jacket. The President looked at us and said: "Do you know that you are putting up a building that will last for three or four hundred years?" We thought that was terrible, but clients always want eternity for buildings like that.

Sculptures by Alberto Giacometti by the water-lily pool.

The Centre Pompidou, designed in 1971, was your first big international success. But it is not a building that might be expected to last for ever. Later buildings like the Beyeler Museum are very reticent in comparison with it. How has this change come about?

It isn't anything to do with change. The brief is completely different in each case. The Beaubourg is a public cultural centre, and Riehen is a private art gallery. In Paris the brief was to conquer new terrain for culture. And besides, museums were not much in demand in the seventies, they were a rather dusty sort of business. No one queued for exhibitions. That was boring. The cultural establishment in Paris intimidated people. That could only be changed by being provocative. An additional feature is that the Centre Pompidou brings a large number of spheres together. For example, over half the visitors use the library. Shortly after completing the Beaubourg I designed the Menil Collection in Houston. It is a real museum, very quiet, a place for contemplation. Without any contamination. There is no break in my architecture here, as there may seem to be from the outside. It is simply that one is very committed to a brief as an architect.

The mass of tubes in Paris embodies the idea of culture as a machine. They were very appropriate to the sixties and early seventies. What would a museum for the next century have to look like?

That brings us very close to the new museum in Riehen. The museum for the next age is a place for preserving and for looking. Very well built. It is a safe, similar to the way the owners of the Florentine palazzi felt, when they started collecting art to protect it from war and damage. They didn't do it to please the public. The palazzi were private places. In a similar way, the Fondation Beyeler museum is in the first place a good instrument for preserving and protecting, and for contemplation. The museum I dream of for the next century is the one that we have just built in Riehen.

The service wing and a porphyry-clad wall border the building on the main road side.

Roof superstructures for the diagonally placed sun awnings.

So how important is art for you when you are developing a museum project?

Art is very important for my work as a whole. It's a very long story. As a young man I was professionally involved in music and fine art. I have worked on a large number of projects involving music and fine art over the years: with Jean Tinguely, Cy Twombly, Roy Lichtenstein, Robert Rauschenberg, with whom I am friendly. He is just producing a large-scale work for a church that I am building in southern Italy. I have similarly strong links with other arts. I am a good friend of Michelangelo Antonioni. I have worked with Pierre Boulez, Luigi Nono and Claudio Abbado. Italo Calvino was a good friend as well. When we were building the Centre Pompidou, he was just writing his "Invisible Cities" book. He looked in on Paris and then devised a city built only by engineers: a city without walls.

You are seen as a high-tech architect. Yet buildings like the Fondation Beyeler museum have an archaic dimension as well. Where do you get your images from?

I find the whole argument about high-tech boring and superfluous. Technology is like a bus to me. I get on it if it's going in the right direction. Otherwise I don't. It would be funny to be living in the year 2000 and not using the instruments that our own age makes available. People have been developing and using techniques from time immemorial. This says absolutely nothing at all about the quality of the interior. The pianist Maurizio Pollini is a good friend of mine. He has an excellent playing technique. But when you listen to him it's hard to say whether it's technique or poetry. The question becomes unimportant. But there can be no poetry without good finger technique.

*The museum opens up to the surrounding landscape
with large glazed façades, here part of a conservatory.*

One of the distinctive features of the Beyeler museum is its relation to nature. What part does balancing nature and technology play in your work?

Architecture is a second nature that we men have made. The story of architecture and building is a story of man's struggle with nature. Our famous friend nature is just lying in wait, ready to kill us as soon as we stop defending ourselves. Technology and nature are in a state of tension with each other. That can be sensed even in the peaceful surroundings of the Beyeler museum. But the tension cannot be broken. We have to endure this complexity.

A complex, multi-layered light ceiling admits changeable daylight to all the exhibition galleries.

So far we have talked about particular buildings. But an architect also takes responsibility for the town; a museum is part of a built environment and its history. For example, you devised the basic concept for the debis buildings in Potsdamer Platz in Berlin. What does your city of the future look like?

I hope that the city of tomorrow will look like the city of yesterday. I don't mean that romantically. It is much more that the European city of the past is a wonderful place. It combines different functions, has cultural wealth, is a place on the right scale, with an urban quality and where people live together. The piazza and the street are wonderful models. We mustn't forget that. We Europeans have built the best cities in the world. But it would be wrong to take up this great tradition in a picturesque fashion, as Prince Charles likes to do.

On entering the park, the museum with four porphyry piers in front of it rises out of a water-lily pond.

Site plan.

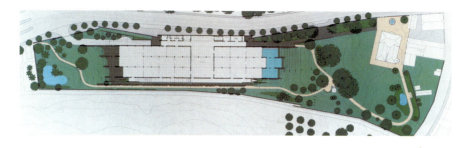

New Museum

Renzo Piano has carefully placed the long museum building in an old park on the edge of the Basel suburb of Riehen. It is concealed by a wall from the busy road. Inside the park, approaching visitors see it rising from a water-lily pool as a pavilion with large glass façades and four porphyry-clad piers. Four reinforced concrete walls 120 m long were placed between the boundary walls of the narrow park, and clad with porphyry on the outside. The supporting figure is an "H"-shape with a double bar. The service wing, through which the museum is entered, has the border wall on the road side behind it. The response to the heavy walls is a filigree roof structure in steel and glass, which filters the daylight with diagonally placed sun-protection panes, double glass ceiling, a layer of slats, perforated metal panels and fabric awnings but at the same time allows it to retain its moods. Under the 4,000 m² roof, 20 galleries are arranged over 2,710 m² on a basic grid of 7 x 11 m in three aisles reminiscent of Louis Kahn's Kimbell Art Museum in Fort Worth, Texas. They are intimate and generous at the same time, and perfectly tailored for the collection of about 180 items, Modern masterpieces and Oceanic sculpture. Signs, monitoring and warning systems were fitted into the walls, the floor is made of French white oak with ventilation channels running through it, and is soundly made; no details break the harmony between the shell of the building and the works exhibited, from van Gogh, Monet and Cézanne via Picasso and Matisse to Kiefer and Baselitz. Large glass façades on the sides and a narrow veranda in front facing west constantly draw the eye into the surrounding fields and park, bringing nature into conversation with art. There is a multi-purpose room in the basement. The offices and cafeteria are accommodated in the 18th-century Villa Berower.

Location
Baselstrasse 77, 4125 Riehen bei Basel, Switzerland, telephone +41 61 645 97 00

Client
Fondation Beyeler Riehen

Project
1992

Construction
1994–1997

Architect
Renzo Piano Building Workshop, Paris/Genoa

Overall co-ordination & site supervision
Burckhardt + Partner, Basel

Structural engineering, building technology, daylight planning
Ove Arup & Partners International, London

Heating, ventilation, air conditioning
Forrer AG

Gross floor area
6,615 m²

Exhibition area
2,710 m²

Gross cubic volume
42,800 m³

Building costs
55 million SFr.

Bibliography
Renzo Piano – Fondation Beyeler. A Home for Art, edited by Fondation Beyeler, Basel/Boston/Berlin 1998.
Renzo Piano Building Workshop, Complete works, edited by Peter Buchanan, vol. 2, London 1996.

East façade on the main road; on the left is the existing building containing the offices.

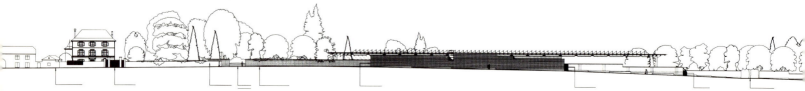

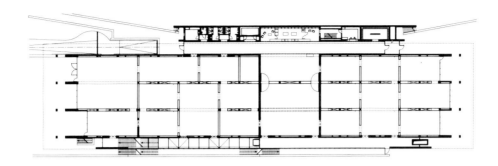

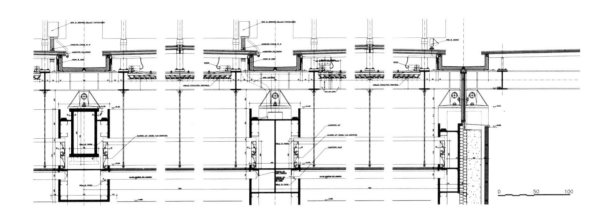

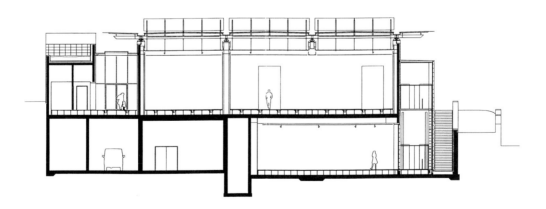

Ground floor plan.

Details of the roof structure.

East-west section.